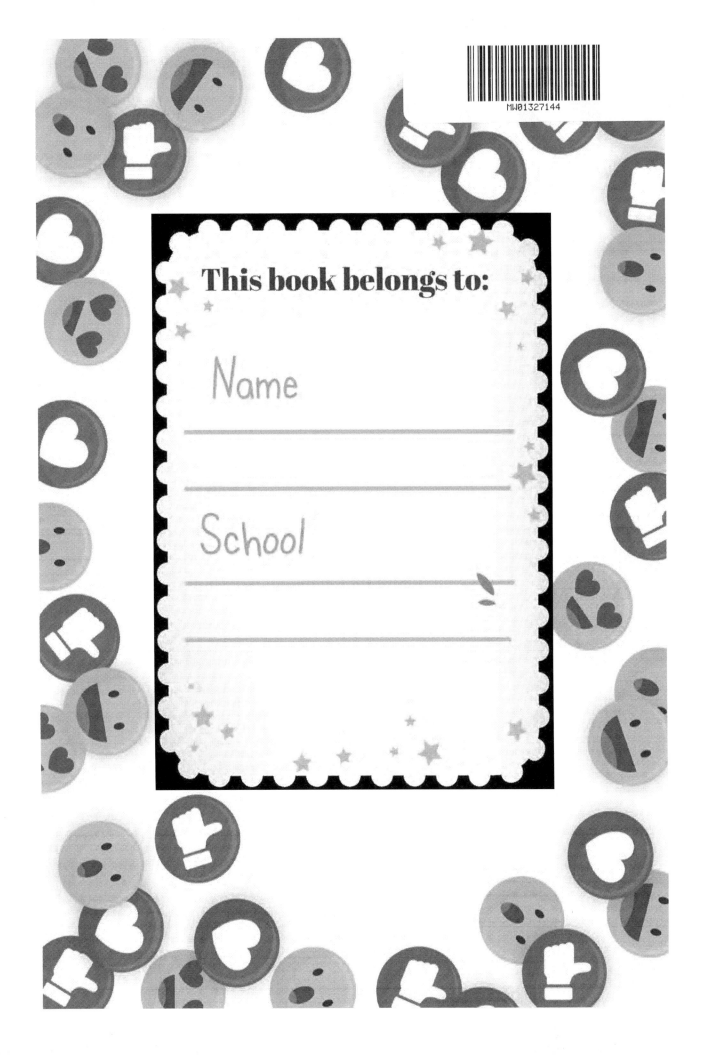

| Full Name | Age & Birthday |
|---|---|
| | |

## ABOUT ME

## Today I am....

☐ Happy  ☐ Bubbly  ☐ Tickled  ☐ Joyous

| QUESTIONS | ANSWERS |
|---|---|
| **Hair Color** | |
| **Eye Color** | |
| **Height** | |
| **Where were you born?** | |
| **Do you have any pets?** | |
| **What is your favorite food?** | |
| **Do you have any brothers and sisters?** | |

What do you want to be when you grow up?

What is your favorite subject in school?

What do you like to do in your free time?

What makes you unique?

# 5th Grade Science: Mallard Duck

Score: _____

Date: _____

First, read the entire passage. After that, go back and fill in the blanks. You can skip the blanks you're unsure about and finish them later.

| plants | habitats | female | bodies | quacking |
| North | hatch | foods | waddle | colors |

The Mallard Duck is what most people think of when they think of ducks. The Mallard is a common duck that can be found throughout _____ America, Europe, and Asia. Central America, Australia, and New Zealand are also home to the Mallard Duck. Anas Platyrhynchos is the scientific name for the Mallard Duck. It belongs to the Dabbling Ducks family. Mallard Ducks enjoy the water and are commonly found near rivers, ponds, and other _____ of water.

Mallard ducks can grow to be about two feet long and weigh about two and a half pounds. The _____ Mallard Duck has tan feathers all over, whereas the male Mallard Duck has a green head, darker back and chest feathers, and a white body. Some people breed domestic Mallard Ducks in order to get different _____.

Mallards are omnivorous birds. This means that they consume both _____ and other animals. They primarily feed on the water's surface, consuming various seeds, small fish, insects, frogs, and fish eggs. They also enjoy some human _____, particularly grain from human crops.

Female Mallard ducks are well-known for their "quack." When you were a kid and learned that ducks make a _____ sound, you were hearing the female Mallard. Females quack to attract other ducks, usually their ducklings. This call is also known as the "hail call" or "decrescendo call." This call can be heard for miles by the ducklings.

Like many other birds, Mallard ducks migrate in flocks from the north to the south for the winter and then back north for the summer. This way, they're always where it's warm, and there's food. These ducks are also adaptable in other ways. They thrive even when humans destroy their natural _____. This is not to say that we should destroy their habitat, but they have not been endangered due to human interaction thus far.

Ducklings are young Mallards. A mother duck will typically lay 10 to 15 eggs. She cares for the eggs in a nest by herself. The mother duck will lead the ducklings to the water shortly after they _____ from the eggs. They usually do not return to the nest after that. Baby ducklings are ready to go just a few hours after hatching. They can swim, _____, feed themselves, and find food quickly. For the next few months, their mother will keep an eye on them and protect them. The ducklings will be able to fly and become self-sufficient after about two months.

# 5th Grade Grammar: Adjectives Matching

Score: _____

Date: _____

Adjectives are words that describe people, places, and things, or nouns. Adjectives are words that describe sounds, shapes, sizes, times, numbers/quantity, textures/touch, and weather. You can remember this by saying to yourself, "an adjective adds something."

If you need to describe a friend or an adult, you can use words that describe their appearance, size, or age. When possible, try to use positive words that describe a person.

|  | |  | |  | |
|---|---|---|---|---|---|
| 1 | ☐ | disappointed | | nothing frightens him/her | A |
| 2 | ☐ | anxious | | everything is in order around him | B |
| 3 | ☐ | delighted | | very pleased | C |
| 4 | ☐ | terrified | | always arrives in time | D |
| 5 | ☐ | ashamed | | loves being with people | E |
| 6 | ☐ | envious | | very surprised and upset | F |
| 7 | ☐ | proud | | very frightened | G |
| 8 | ☐ | shocked | | wanting something another person has | H |
| 9 | ☐ | brave | | feeling bad because you did sg wrong | I |
| 10 | ☐ | hard-working | | uprightness and fairness | J |
| 11 | ☐ | organized | | worried | K |
| 12 | ☐ | punctual | | has 2 or more jobs | L |
| 13 | ☐ | honest | | always supports his friends | M |
| 14 | ☐ | outgoing | | feeling pleased and satisfied | N |
| 15 | ☐ | loyal | | sad because something is worse than expected | O |
| 16 | ☐ | reliable | | one can always count on him | P |

# 5th Grade Grammar Review

Score: _____

Date: _____

Common & Proper Noun: A noun is a word that is used to describe a person, animal, place, thing, or idea. **Common nouns** are words that are used to refer to general objects rather than specific ones. All of these items are named with common nouns: lamp, chair, couch, TV, window, painting, pillow, and candle.

A **proper noun** is a unique (not generic) name for a specific person, place, or thing. In English, proper nouns are always capitalized, regardless of where they appear in a sentence.

**Common noun:** I want to be a **writer**. ✓
**Proper noun: Carlyon Jones** wrote many books. ✓

**Plural Nouns: Plural nouns** are words that indicate the presence of more than one person, animal, place, thing, or idea.

- bottle – bottles. ✓
- cup – cups. ✓

**Collective Nouns: Collective nouns** are names for a collection or a number of people or things.

crowd, government, team, family, audience, etc.

**Singular Possessive Noun:** A **singular possessive noun** indicates that something is owned by someone or something. We add an's to indicate ownership. • *cat's tail*, for example.

**Concrete Noun:** A **concrete noun** is a real-world physical object, such as a dog, a ball, or an ice cream cone. Another way to put it, a concrete noun is the name of an object which may be perceived by one or more of the five senses. An **abstract noun** is a concept or idea that does not exist in the physical world and cannot be touched, such as freedom, sadness, or permission.

**Verb:** A verb is defined as a word (such as jump, think, happen, or exist) that expresses an action and is usually one of the main parts of a sentence.

**Adjectives** are words that describe the qualities or states of being of nouns: enormous, doglike, silly, yellow, fun, fast.

**Simple Subject:** A **simple subject** is a subject's main word or words. It lacks any modifiers that could be used to describe the subject. To find the simple subject in a sentence, consider who or what is doing the action in the sentence. But keep in mind that a simple subject is very basic, a subject, a verb, and a completed thought.

Tina waited for the train.
"Tina" = subject, "waited" = verb ✓

**Prepositions Object:** A preposition is a word that appears before a noun to indicate its relationship to another word in the phrase or clause.
As a result, a noun can serve as the object of the preposition. The noun that follows the preposition is known as the object of the preposition.

To find the preposition's object:

1) Locate the preposition.
2) Then, put the preposition in the blank and ask "_____ who or what?"

Jim's house is across the street. (Across what?) street ✓
The show will begin at 7:00. (At what?) 7:00 ✓

**Indirect Object:** An indirect object is one that is used with a transitive verb to indicate who benefits from or receives something as a result of an action. In the sentence 'She gave him her address,' for example, 'him' is the indirect object.

**Direct object:** A direct object is a word or phrase that receives the verb's action. The direct object in the sentence: 'The kids eat cake.' is cake; the verb is eat, and the object being eaten is cake.

**Direct Address:** Nouns of **direct address** are the nouns used to indicate that a speaker is directly addressing a person or group. When addressing a person or thing directly, the name must be separated by a comma (or commas if in the middle of a sentence).

- Tommy, are you leaving so soon? ✓ (As "Tommy" is being addressed directly, his name is offset with a comma.)

1. His father is the coach of the team.
    a. his, father, team
    b. his, father, coach
    c. father, coach, team

2. David is driving to the beach.
    a. David, driving, beach
    b. David, driving
    c. David, beach

3. What are the PROPER nouns in the following sentence? My grandparents live in Florida.
    a. grandparents, Flordia
    b. Flordia
    c. My, grandparents

4. What are all the COMMON nouns in the following sentence? I have two dogs and one cat.
    a. cat, one
    b. dogs, cat
    c. I, dogs

5. Which sentence contains only one common noun and one proper noun?
    a. These potatoes are from Idaho.
    b. Casey is a talented singer and dancer.
    c. I live near the border of Nevada and Utah.

6. Which sentence contains the correct form of a plural noun?
    a. The wolves chase a frightened rabbit.
    b. The wolfes chase a frightened rabbit.
    c. The wolfs chase a frightened rabbit.

7. Which sentence contains one singular noun and one plural noun?
    a. The musician tunes her instrument.
    b. The conductor welcomes each musician.
    c. The singers walk across the stage.

8. Identify the collective noun in the following sentence.
   Derek is the lead singer in a band.
    a. singer
    b. band
    c. lead

9. Which sentence contains the correct form of a singular possessive noun?
    a. The boxs' lid is torn.
    b. The box's lid is torn.
    c. The boxes' lid is torn.

10. Which sentence contains one concrete noun and on abstract noun?
    a. John feels anxiety about meeting new people.
    b. The young boy plays with trains.
    c. The sand feels warm between my toes.

11. Identify the simple subject in the following sentence.      The children are playing tag.
    a. tag
    b. children
    c. The children

12. Identify the simple subject in the following sentence. This computer belongs to my father.
    a. computer
    b. This computer
    c. father

13. Which sentence has an object of a preposition?
    a. Several passengers missed the flight.
    b. Seattle is a city in Washington.
    c. The boys are racing remote-controlled cars.

14. Identify the object of preposition in the following sentence. The are playing a game of cards.
    a. cards
    b. game
    c. of cards

15. Identify the subject complement in the following sentence. Mr. Smith is a talented poet.
    a. poet
    b. talented
    c. Mr. Smith

16. Identify the subject complement in the following sentence. Tulips and daisies are my favorite flowers.
    a. my
    b. flowers
    c. favorite

17. Identify the direct object in the following sentence.      Tyler delivers newspapers each morning.
    a. newspapers
    b. morning
    c. each

18. Identify the direct object in the following sentence.      We will paint the bathroom beige.
    a. bathroom
    b. paint
    c. beige

19. Identify the indirect object in the following sentence.      Mr. Jackson gave the students their grades.
    a. grades
    b. students
    c. their

20. Identify the indirect object in the following sentence.      Mrs. Parker bought her husband a new tie.
    a. new tie
    b. husband
    c. tie

21. In which sentence is paint used as a noun?
    a. These artists paint the most amazing murals.
    b. We need two cans of brown paint.
    c. Let's paint the bedroom light green.

22. In which sentence is sign used as a verb?
    a. I saw it as a sign of good luck.
    b. Joelle is learning sign language.
    c. Did you sign the letter at the bottom?

23. In which sentence is file used as an adjective?
    a. This file contains the detective's notes.
    b. Put these papers in a file folder.
    c. I use a file to smooth the edges of my nails.

24. Identify the direct address in the following sentence. This is your baseball bat, Kenny.
    a. Kenny
    b. baseball
    c. bat

25. Identify the direct address in the following sentence.
    Hector, did you buy more milk?
    a. Hector
    b. you
    c. milk

26. Objects of the preposition. Lee cried during the movie.
    a. Lee
    b. movie
    c. cried

27. Objects of the preposition. The phone is on the table.
    a. table
    b. phone
    c. none

28. Direct Objects: Every actor played his part.
    a. his part
    b. actor
    c. played

29. Direct Objects: The crowd will cheer the President.
    a. the President
    b. cheer
    c. crowd

30. Examples of concrete nouns are:
    a. flower, music, bear, pie,
    b. love, cars, them, went
    c. me, I, she, they

31. Direct Address: Well certainly, Mother, I remember what you said.
    a. you
    b. Mother
    c. certainly

32. Direct Address: I heard exactly what you said, Pam.
    a. Pam
    b. none
    c. you

33. Collective Noun: A choir of singers
    a. choir
    b. sing
    c. singers

34. Collective Noun: A litter of puppies
    a. litter
    b. puppies
    c. puppy

# 5th Grade Grammar: IRREGULAR VERBS

Score: _____

Date: _____

Irregular past tense verbs are those that are formed in a way that does not follow the '-ed' pattern, such as jump/jumped. Some are more straightforward than others:

She eats. (present tense)
She ate. (past tense)

It can be difficult to use irregular past tense verbs at times. Even after teaching the distinction between 'lie' and 'lay,' teachers frequently have to look up the correct irregular past tense before writing it!

1. **Jen has (go) to the same school since first grade.**
   a. gone
   b. goned

2. **When she was 17, she (wrote) a book.**
   a. wrote
   b. written

3. **Rees´ mother (drive) them to the cinema.**
   a. drove
   b. drived

4. **begin**
   a. began
   b. begins

5. **The pitcher (throw) a no-hitter yesterday.**
   a. thrown
   b. threw

6. **bear**
   a. bore
   b. beard

7. **After practice, they (take) us to dinner.**
   a. tooked
   b. took

8. **They (become) best friends in the fourth grade.**
   a. began
   b. became

9. **burnt**
   a. burn
   b. burns

10. **break**
    a. broke
    b. brokes

11. **caught**
    a. catches
    b. catch

12. **The boy (say) that his name was Jim.**
    a. says
    b. said

13. **The Titanic had (sink) by the time the rescue boats arrived.**
    a. sinked
    b. sunk

14. **The cartoon character had (shrink) to the size of a mouse.**
    a. shrinked
    b. shrunk

15. creep
    a. creeps
    b. crept

17. dream
    a. dreamt
    b. dreams

19. fall
    a. falled
    b. fell

21. Speak
    a. irregular
    b. regular

23. go
    a. regular
    b. irregular

25. Love
    a. regular
    b. irregular

27. work
    a. regular
    b. irregular

29. Create
    a. irregular
    b. regular

31. I (make) my mom a cake.
    a. makes
    b. made

33. One day, he (see) a new student on the bus.
    a. sees
    b. saw

35. They (go) to six movies last summer.
    a. gone
    b. went

16. Ree and Jim have (know) each other for two years.
    a. known
    b. knewed

18. Have you ever (wear) a cowboy hat?
    a. worn
    b. worned

20. After practice, they (take) us to dinner.
    a. taken
    b. took

22. travel
    a. regular
    b. irregular

24. Come
    a. irregular
    b. regular

26. Become
    a. regular
    b. irregular

28. read
    a. irregular
    b. regular

30. We (bring) my dog to the park.
    a. brought
    b. brung

32. We (drink) all the water.
    a. drinks
    b. drunk

34. The two boys have also (see) many movies together.
    a. looked
    b. seen

36. Have you ever (wear) a cowboy hat?
    a. weared
    b. worn

# 5th Grade Grammar: Singular and Plural

Score: _____

Date: _____

Nouns can take many different forms. Singular and plural are two of these forms. A singular noun refers to a single person, place, thing, or idea. A plural noun is one that refers to two or more people, places, things, or ideas. How do you pluralize a singular noun? Making a singular noun plural is usually as simple as adding a **s** to the end of the word.
Example: Singular toy | Plural toys

Some nouns, however, do not follow this rule and are referred to as irregular nouns. How do I pluralize a singular irregular noun?

We'll start with **singular nouns** that end in s, ss, ch, sh, x, or z. If a singular noun **ends in s, ss, ch, sh, x, or z**, add **es** at the end.
**Example: beach--->beaches**

If the singular noun **ends in a vowel**, the letters a, e, I o, and u are usually suffixed with an **s**.
**Example: video--->videos**

If a singular noun **ends with a consonant + o**, it is common to add an **es** at the end. Except for a, e, I o, and u, consonants are all the letters of the alphabet.
**Example: potato--->potatoes**

Simply add a **s** to the end of the word if the singular noun **ends in a vowel + y** pattern.
**Example: day--->days**

Now we'll look at singular nouns that **end in f or fe**. If the singular noun ends in a f or fe, **change it to a v and then add es**.
**Example: life--->lives**

Consonant + y is another unusual noun. If the singular noun **ends with a consonant + y** pattern, **change the y to I before adding es**.
**Example: bunny---> bunnies**

Some nouns are spelled the same way in both the singular and plural forms.

It's now time to make some spelling changes. When you switch from the singular to plural form of a noun, the spelling changes. The following are some examples of common words that change spelling when formed into plurals:
**Example: child--->childrens**

Select the best answer for each question.

1. Which word is NOT a plural noun?
   a. books
   b. hat
   c. toys

2. Which word is a singular noun?
   a. bikes
   b. cars
   c. pencil

3. Which word can be both singular and plural?
   a. deer
   b. bears
   c. mice

4. Tommy _____ badminton at the court.
   a. playing
   b. plays
   c. play's

5. They _____ to eat at fast food restaurants once in a while.
   a. likes
   b. like
   c. likies

6. Everybody _____ Janet Jackson.
   a. know
   b. known
   c. knows

7. He ___ very fast. You have to listen carefully.
    a. spoken
    b. speak
    c. speaks

8. Which one is the singular form of women?
    a. womans
    b. woman
    c. women

9. The plural form of tooth is
    a. tooths
    b. toothes
    c. teeth

10. The singular form of mice is _____.
    a. mouse
    b. mices
    c. mouses

11. The plural form of glass is _____.
    a. glassies
    b. glasses
    c. glassy

12. The plural form of dress is _____.
    a. dressing
    b. dresses
    c. dressy

13. Plural means many.
    a. True
    b. False

14. Singular means 1.
    a. True
    b. False

15. Is this word singular or plural? monsters
    a. plural
    b. singular

16. Find the plural noun in the sentence. They gave her a nice vase full of flowers.
    a. they
    b. flowers
    c. vase

17. Find the plural noun in the sentence. Her baby brother grabbed the crayons out of the box and drew on the wall.
    a. crayons
    b. box
    c. brothers

18. Find the plural noun in the sentence. My friend, Lois, picked enough red strawberries for the whole class.
    a. strawberries
    b. friends
    c. classes

19. What is the correct plural form of the noun wish?
    a. wishes
    b. wishs
    c. wishy

20. What is the correct plural form of the noun flurry?
    a. flurrys
    b. flurryies
    c. flurries

21. What is the correct plural form of the noun box?
    a. boxs
    b. boxses
    c. boxes

22. What is the correct plural form of the noun bee?
    a. beess
    b. beeses
    c. bees

23. What is the correct plural form of the noun candy?
    a. candys
    b. candyies
    c. candies

24. Find the singular noun in the sentence. The boys and girls drew pictures on the sidewalk.
    a. boys
    b. drew
    c. sidewalk

Rounding rules:

Look at the digit to the right to round a number to the nearest ten place. If the number is five or more, round up. If the number is four or less, round down.

Round up if a number ends in 5, 6, 7, 8, or 9.
Round down if a number ends in 1, 2, 3, or 4.

For instance, 671 rounded to the nearest ten is 670 because the digit to the right of the tens place ended with one, so we round down.

Score : _____

Date : _____

## Round each number to the nearest tens.

1)    712  ⟶  710
      - 397  ⟶  - 400
                        310

2)    428  ⟶
      - 232  ⟶  - _____

3)    716  ⟶
      + 479  ⟶  + _____

4)    514  ⟶
      + 133  ⟶  + _____

5)    935  ⟶
      - 188  ⟶  - _____

6)    481  ⟶
      + 131  ⟶  + _____

7)    798  ⟶
      - 647  ⟶  - _____

8)    484  ⟶
      + 235  ⟶  + _____

9)    939  ⟶
      + 548  ⟶  + _____

10)    692  ⟶
       + 542  ⟶  + _____

11)    414  ⟶
       + 921  ⟶  + _____

12)    224  ⟶
       - 154  ⟶  - _____

13)    321  ⟶
       - 257  ⟶  - _____

14)    295  ⟶
       - 182  ⟶  - _____

Multiply the length by the conversion ratio to convert a foot measurement to an inch measurement. Because one foot equals 12 inches, you can use the following simple formula to convert: inches = feet × 12. For example, using the formula above, here's how to convert 5 feet to inches. 5' = (5 × 12) = 60"

Score : _____

Date : _____

## Converting Feet and Inches
### Convert to Inches.

1)  4 feet   11 inches   __59 inches__     5)  15 feet   9 inches   _____

    4X12=48+11=59

2)  8 feet   4 inches   _____     6)  13 feet   7 inches   _____

3)  4 feet   6 inches   _____     7)  7 feet   6 inches   _____

4)  14 feet   5 inches   _____     8)  4 feet   3 inches   _____

Convert inches to feet and inches with this simple formula:
feet = inches ÷ 12

### Convert to Feet and Inches.

9)  __5 FEET 1 INCH__   61 inches     13)  _____   57 inches

10)  _____   112 inches     14)  _____   21 inches

11)  _____   138 inches     15)  _____   163 inches

12)  _____   129 inches     16)  _____   190 inches

# Time

Score : _____
Date : _____

What time is on the clock? _____

What time will it be in 4 hours and 20 minutes? _____

What time was it 1 hour and 40 minutes ago? _____

What time will it be in 3 hours ? _____

What time is on the clock? _____

What time will it be in 1 hour and 40 minutes? _____

What time was it 2 hours and 20 minutes ago? _____

What time will it be in 1 hour ? _____

What time is on the clock? _____

What time will it be in 3 hours and 40 minutes? _____

What time was it 1 hour and 20 minutes ago? _____

What time will it be in 4 hours ? _____

What time is on the clock? _____

What time will it be in 4 hours ? _____

What time was it 2 hours and 20 minutes ago? _____

What time will it be in 2 hours ? _____

# 5th Grade History: The Mayflower

Score: _____

Date: _____

First, read the entire passage. After that, go back and fill in the blanks. You can skip the blanks you're unsure about and finish them later.

| ship | sail | voyage | assist | settlers |
| passengers | illness | load | leaking | Cape |

In 1620, a _____ called the Mayflower transported a group of English colonists to North America. These people established New England's first permanent European colony in what is now Plymouth, Massachusetts. Later, they were named the Pilgrims.

The Mayflower was approximately 106 feet long, 25 feet wide, and had a tonnage of 180. The deck of the Mayflower was about 80 feet long, roughly the length of a basketball court. The ship had three masts for holding sails:

The fore-mast (in front)

The main-mast (in the middle)

The mizzen mast (in the back) (back)

On August 4, 1620, the Mayflower and the Speedwell set sail from Southampton, England. They had to come to a halt in Dartmouth, however, because the Speedwell was leaking. They left Dartmouth on August 21, but the Speedwell began _____ again, and they came to a halt in Plymouth, England. They decided to abandon the Speedwell at Plymouth and _____ as many passengers as possible onto the Mayflower. On September 6, 1620, they set sail from Plymouth.

The Mayflower set _____ from Plymouth, England, west across the Atlantic Ocean. The ship's original destination was Virginia, but storms forced it to change course. On November 9, 1620, more than two months after leaving Plymouth, the Mayflower sighted _____ Cod. The Pilgrims decided to stay even though they were north of where they had planned to settle.

It is estimated that around 30 children were on board the Mayflower during the epic _____ to America, but little is known about many of them.

They were children of passengers, some traveled with other adults, and some were servants - but having young people among the _____ was critical to the Plymouth Colony's survival.

It is believed that when the colonists faced their first harsh winter of _____ and death in a new land, the children would _____ the adults by tending to the sick, assisting in the preparation of food, and fetching firewood and water.

While nearly half of the ship's _____ died during the winter of 1620/1621, it is believed that there were fewer deaths among the children, implying that the struggling colony had a better chance of thriving.

# 5th Grade History: Native American Princess Pocahontas

Score: _____

Date: _____

First, read the entire passage. After that, go back and fill in the blanks. You can skip the blanks you're unsure about and finish them later.

| freedom | ransom | gravely | chief | princess |
| Jamestown | thatch | captured | spare | accident |

Pocahontas was the daughter of the Powhatan _____. Historians place her birth in the year 1595. Her father was not only the chief of a tiny tribe; he was also the chief of a big confederation of Native American tribes that occupied a considerable portion of eastern Virginia.

Despite her status as the chief's daughter, Pocahontas' childhood was likely similar to that of most Native American girls. She would have lived in a _____ roof house, learned to build a fire and cook, foraged for food in the woods such as berries and nuts, and played games with other children.

When Pocahontas was about twelve years old, strange strangers from a distant land arrived. They were colonists of the English language. They founded _____ on an island near the Powhatan lands. The Powhatan's interaction with the outsiders was uneasy. They traded with strangers at times and fought them at others.

Captain John Smith, the Jamestown settlement's captain, was _____ by some of her father's warriors one day. According to mythology, Chief Powhatan was about to assassinate John Smith when Pocahontas rescued him. She pleaded with her father to _____ the life of Smith. Her father consented, and Captain Smith was released.

After Pocahontas saved John Smith, the Powhatan's relationship with the settlers improved. They traded with one another, and Pocahontas frequently paid visits to the Jamestown fort to speak with John Smith. In 1609, after being injured in a gunpowder _____, John Smith was forced to return to England. The Powhatan's relationship with the settlers deteriorated once more.

English Captain Samuel Argall captured Pocahontas in 1613. He informed Pocahontas' father that he intended to exchange her for the _____ of other English captives held by the Powhatan. The two parties engaged in lengthy negotiations. Pocahontas met and fell in love with tobacco farmer John Rolfe while imprisoned. Even though her father had paid the _____, she chose to remain with the English. On April 5, 1614, at the chapel in Jamestown, she married John Rolfe. She gave birth to a son called Thomas around a year later.

Pocahontas and John Rolfe sailed to London a few years after their marriage. Pocahontas was treated like a _____ while in London. She wore ostentatious gowns, attended extravagant parties, and met King James I of England. She even met John Smith, whom she had assumed was dead.

Pocahontas and John Rolfe intended to return to Virginia through the sea. Regrettably, Pocahontas fell _____ ill as they prepared to depart sail. She died in Gravesend, England, in March 1617.

# 5th Grade History: The Thirteen Colonies

Score: _____

Date: _____

In 1776, thirteen British colonies merged to form the United States. Many of these colonies had existed for well over a century, including Virginia's first colony, founded in 1607.

A colony is a region of land that is politically controlled by another country. As was the case with England and the American colonies, the controlling country is usually physically distant from the colony. Colonies are typically founded and settled by people from the home country, but settlers from other countries may also be present. This was especially true of the American colonies, which people from all over Europe populated.

Here is a list of the thirteen colonies, along with the year they were established () and a description of how they were established.

**Virginia:** John Smith and the London Company set out for Virginia in 1607.

**New York:** The Dutch founded New York in 1626. In 1664, it became a British colony.

**New Hampshire:** John Mason was the first landholder in New Hampshire (1623). Eventually, John Wheelwright.

**Massachusetts Bay:** Puritans seeking religious freedom in Massachusetts Bay (1630).

**Maryland** (1633) - George and Cecil Calvert established it as a safe haven for Catholics.

**Connecticut** (1636) - Thomas Hooker, who had been ordered to leave Massachusetts.

**Rhode Island**: Roger Williams founded Rhode Island (1636) to provide a place of religious freedom for all.

**Delaware**: Peter Minuit and the New Sweden Company founded Delaware in 1638. In 1664, the British took over.

**North Carolina** (1663) - Originally a part of the Carolina Province. Separated from South Carolina in 1712.

**South Carolina** (1663) - Originally a part of the Carolina Province. In 1712, South Carolina seceded from North Carolina.

**New Jersey** (1664) - Initially settled by the Dutch, the English took control in 1664.

**Pennsylvania** (1681) William Penn and the Quakers.

**Georgia** (1732) - James Oglethorpe as a debtor's settlement.

Queen Elizabeth desired to establish colonies in the Americas to expand the British Empire and compete with the Spanish. The English hoped to find riches, create new jobs, and develop trade ports along the Americas' coasts.

Each colony, on the other hand, has its distinct history of how it was founded. Many of the colonies were established by religious leaders or groups seeking religious liberty. Pennsylvania, Massachusetts, Maryland, Rhode Island, and Connecticut were among these colonies. Other colonies were established solely to create new trade opportunities and profits for investors.

The colonies are frequently divided into New England Colonies, Middle Colonies, and Southern Colonies.

**New England Colonies:** Connecticut, Massachusetts Bay, New Hampshire, Rhode Island

**Middle Colonies:** Delaware, New Jersey, New York, Pennsylvania

**Southern Colonies:** Georgia, Maryland, North Carolina, South Carolina, Virginia

1. **The Dutch founded _____ in 1626.**
   a. New Jersey
   b. New York

2. **13 British colonies merged to form the _____.**
   a. United Kingdom
   b. United States

3. **Roger Williams founded _____.**
   a. Maryland
   b. Rhode Island

4. **A colony is a region of _____ that is politically controlled by another country.**
   a. land
   b. township

5. **Middle Colonies:**
   a. Delaware, New Jersey, New York, Pennsylvania
   b. Georgia, Maryland, North Carolina, South Carolina, Texas

6. **Colonies are typically founded and settled by people from the ___ country.**
   a. home
   b. outside

7. **Southern Colonies:**
   a. Maine, New Jersey, New York, Pennsylvania
   b. Georgia, Maryland, North Carolina, South Carolina, Virginia

8. **Many of the colonies were established by ____ leaders or groups seeking religious liberty.**
   a. political
   b. religious

9. **New England Colonies:**
   a. Connecticut, Massachusetts Bay, New Hampshire, Rhode Island
   b. Ohio, Tennessee, New York, Pennsylvania

10. **George and Cecil Calvert established _____ as a safe haven for Catholics.**
    a. Maine
    b. Maryland

11. **The colonies are frequently divided into _____.**
    a. New England Colonies, Middle Colonies, and Southern Colonies
    b. United England Colonies, Midland Colonies, and Southern Colonies.

# Understanding Questions- Answer Relationship

Score: _____

Date: _____

The question-answer relationship (QAR) strategy helps students understand the different types of questions. By learning that the answers to some questions are "Right There" in the text, that some answers require a reader to "Think and Search," and that some answers can only be answered "On My Own," students recognize that they must first consider the question before developing an answer.

Throughout your education, you may be asked four different types of questions on a quiz:

**Right There Questions:** Literal questions with answers in the text. The words used in the question are frequently the same as those found in the text.

**Think and Search Questions**: Answers are obtained from various parts of the text and combined to form meaning.

**The Author and You:** These questions are based on information from the text, but you must apply it to your own experience. Although the answer is not directly in the text, you must have read it in order to respond to the question.

**On My Own:** These questions may require you to do some research outside of reading the passage. You can use primary sources to help such as online research articles, books, historical documents, and autobiographies.

**Why is the question-answer relationship used?**

It has the potential to improve your reading comprehension.
It teaches you how to ask questions about what you're reading and where to look for answers.
It encourages you to think about the text you're reading as well as beyond it.
It motivates you to think creatively and collaboratively, while also challenging you to use higher-level thinking skills.

1. Literal questions with answers in the text are_____.
    a. Right There Questions
    b. Right Here Questions

2. These questions are based on information from the text, but you must apply it to your own
    a. The Teacher and You
    b. The Author and You

3. Answers are obtained from various parts of the text.
    a. Think and Search Questions
    b. Check Your Knowledge Questions

4. These questions may require you to do some research outside of reading the passage.
    a. On My Own
    b. Find The Author

# 5th Grade Science Multiple Choice Quiz: Tyrannosaurus Rex

Score: _____

Date: _____

Tyrannosaurus Rex, one of the most famous and notable dinosaurs, is a theropod dinosaur. Many Tyrannosaurus fossils have been discovered, allowing scientists to learn more about how big it was, how it hunted, and how it lived.

Tyrannosaurus rex was a land predator dinosaur that was one of the largest. The T-rex could grow to be 43 feet long and weigh up to 7.5 tons. Because of its size and overall fearsome image, the dinosaur is frequently used in movies and films such as Jurassic Park.

Tyrannosaurus rex was a two-legged dinosaur. This means it could walk and run on two legs. These two legs were large and strong enough to support the dinosaur's massive weight. The T-arms, rex's, on the other hand, were relatively small. However, it is believed that the small arms were powerful to hold onto prey.

The Tyrannosaurus' massive skull and large teeth are among its most terrifying features. T-rex skulls as long as 5 feet have been discovered! Other evidence suggests that the Tyrannosaurus had a powerful bite that allowed it to crush other dinosaurs' bones easily when combined with sharp teeth.

The Tyrannosaurus Rex ate meat from other animals and dinosaurs. Still, it is unclear whether it was a predator (hunted and killed its food) or a scavenger (meaning it stole food from other predators). Many scientists believe the dinosaur did both. Much is dependent on how fast the dinosaur was. Some claim that the T-Rex was fast and capable of catching its prey. Others argue that the dinosaur was slow and used its fearsome jaws to frighten other predators and steal their prey.

There are numerous significant Tyrannosaurus specimens in museums around the world. "Sue" at the Field Museum of Natural History in Chicago is one of the largest and most comprehensive. "Stan," another significant T-Rex specimen, can be found at the Black Hills Museum of Natural History Exhibit in Hill City, South Dakota. Also on display at the American Museum of Natural History in New York, paleontologist Barnum Brown's largest Tyrannosaurus find (he discovered five in total). The only known Tyrannosaurus Rex track can be found at Philmont Scout Ranch in New Mexico.

---

Remember that there may be some **question-answer relationship (QAR)** questions, so please keep that in mind when answering the questions below.

1. The T-rex usually measures up to _____ and weighs as much as _____.
   a. 43 feet, 2 tons
   b. 43 feet, 7.5 tons

2. The Tyrannosaurus rex was a _____ dinosaur.
   a. quadrupedal
   b. bipedal

3. The T-rex is a member of the dinosaur subgroup _____, which includes all the flesh-eating dinosaurs.
   a. Thyreophora
   b. Theropoda

4. The Tyrannosaurus rex lived in North America between 65 and 98 million years ago, during the late _____ period.
   a. Cretaceous
   b. Triassic

5. Where could we find the only documented track of a Tyrannosaurus Rex?
   a. at Philmont Scout Ranch in New Mexico
   b. at the Field Museum of Natural History in Chicago

6. Which of the following is the largest and most complete T-rex specimen that can be found on display at the Field Museum of Natural History in Chicago?
   a. Stan
   b. Sue

7. The Tyrannosaurus had a life span of around _____.
   a. 30 years
   b. 50 years

8. It is one of the most ferocious predators to ever walk the Earth.
   a. Giganotosaurus
   b. Tyrannosaurus rex

9. Tyrannosaurus rex was also adept at finding its prey through its keen sense of _____.
   a. smell
   b. sight

10. Tyrannosaurus rex (rex meaning "_____" in Latin).
    a. king
    b. master

# 5th Grade Biography 30th U.S. President: Calvin Coolidge

Calvin Coolidge is well-known for cleaning up after his predecessor, President Harding. He's also known for being a man of few words, earning him the moniker "Silent Cal."

Calvin grew up in the small Vermont town of Plymouth. Calvin's father was a storekeeper who instilled in him puritan values such as frugality, hard work, and honesty. Calvin was a quiet but hardworking young man. Calvin attended Amherst College before relocating to Massachusetts to pursue a law degree. He passed the bar exam and became a lawyer in 1897, opening his law firm a year later. Calvin also worked in various city offices over the next few years before meeting and marrying Grace Goodhue, a schoolteacher, in 1905.

Before becoming president, Coolidge held several elected positions. He was a city councilman and a solicitor in his hometown. He later became a state legislator and the mayor of Northampton. He was then elected as Massachusetts' lieutenant governor, and in 1918, he was elected as the state's governor. During the 1919 Boston Police Strike, Coolidge gained national attention as governor of Massachusetts. This was when the Boston police officers formed a union and decided to strike or not show up for work. With no cops on the beat, Boston's streets became dangerous. Coolidge went on the offensive, fired the strikers, and hired a new police force. Coolidge was unexpectedly chosen as Warren Harding's vice-presidential running mate in 1920. They won the election, and Coolidge was appointed as Vice President.

President Harding died on a trip to Alaska in 1923. Harding's administration was riddled with corruption and scandal. Coolidge, fortunately, had not been a part of the corruption and immediately cleaned the house. He fired corrupt and inept officials and replaced them with new, dependable employees.

Calvin Coolidge's quiet but honest demeanor appeared to be exactly what the country needed at the time. The economy thrived as a result of cleaning up the scandals and showing support for businesses. This prosperous era became known as the "Roaring Twenties." Coolidge was elected president for a second term after Harding's term ended. He campaigned with the slogan "Keep Cool with Coolidge." Coolidge, as president, advocated for limited government. He also desired to keep the country somewhat isolated and refused to join the League of Nations, which was formed following World War I. He advocated for tax cuts, reduced government spending, and less assistance to struggling farmers. In 1928, Coolidge decided not to run for president again. Although he was likely to win, he felt he had served his time as president.

In 1928, Coolidge decided not to run for president again. Although he was likely to win, he felt he had served his time as president.

---

Remember that there may be some question-answer relationship (QAR) questions, so please keep that in mind when answering the questions below.

1. **Calvin Coolidge was the _____ of the United States.**
   a. 30th President
   b. 31st President
   c. 29th President

2. **Calvin Coolidge served as President from _____ to _____.**
   a. 1923-1929
   b. 1929-1933
   c. 1913-1921

3. **He is also famous for _____ earning him the nickname _____.**
   a. breaking up large companies, The Trust Buster
   b. bing excellent in academic, schoolmaster
   c. being a man of few words, Silent Cal

4. **Calvin grew up in the small town of _____.**
   a. Plymouth, Vermont
   b. Staunton, Virginia
   c. New York, New York

5. Calvin Coolidge signed the _____, which gave full U.S. citizen rights to all Native Americans.
    a. The Dawes Act
    b. Indian Citizenship Act
    c. Indian Civil Rights Act

6. Who was the Vice President under Calvin Coolidge's administration?
    a. Charles Curtis
    b. Thomas Riley Sherman
    c. Charles Gates Dawes

7. Coolidge gained national recognition during the 1919 _____ when he served as governor.
    a. Boston Police Strike
    b. Baltimore Police Strike
    c. NYPD Police Strike

8. Calvin died of a sudden heart attack _____ years after leaving the presidency.
    a. five
    b. three
    c. four

9. Calvin Coolidge became President of the United States after his predecessor, _____ died in office.
    a. Warren Harding
    b. William Taft
    c. Herbert Hoover

10. The _____ is a nickname for the 1920s in the United States as it was a time of hope, prosperity, and cultural change during President Calvin Coolidge's presidential term.
    a. Roaring Twenties
    b. Gilded Age
    c. Reconstruction

11. Which of the following words best describes President Calvin Coolidge's personality?
    a. quiet
    b. adventurous
    c. talkative

12. What was Calvin Coolidge's campaign slogan when he ran for President of the United States?
    a. Keep Cool with Coolidge
    b. Coolidge, For the Future
    c. Peace, Prosperity, and Coolidge

Calvin Coolidge was an American lawyer and politician who served as the country's 30th president from 1923 to 1929. Coolidge, a Republican lawyer from New England who was born in Vermont, rose through the ranks of Massachusetts state politics to become the state's governor.

# 5th Grade Biography American Aviator: Charles Lindbergh

On February 4, 1902, Charles Lindbergh was born in Detroit, Michigan. When Charles was a child, his father was elected to the United States Congress. His mother worked as a teacher. Charles spent a large part of his childhood in Minnesota and Washington, D.C. He enjoyed being outside while growing up on his family's farm in Minnesota.

Charles aspired to be a pilot one day. He dropped out of the University of Wisconsin after two years to work as an airplane mechanic. Then he took flying lessons and began flying barnstormers. Barnstormers were air show pilots who traveled the country performing stunts and giving people rides.

Charles joined the Army Air Service in 1924, where he received formal pilot training. He became a mail pilot after graduating from the army's training school. This was a dangerous job at the time because pilots had to navigate primarily by sight and had no way of knowing when they were flying into bad weather.

For years, Charles had hoped to win the Orteig Prize, which awarded $25,000 to the first pilot to fly nonstop from New York to Paris. The prize was first offered in 1919, but no one had completed the flight by 1927. Charles was confident that he could complete the flight. He persuaded several St. Louis businessmen to contribute to the construction of a particular plane.

Charles took off from New York in his plane, the Spirit of St. Louis, on May 20, 1927. Charles flew the plane towards Paris for the next 33 1/2 hours. It was a perilous flight. When possible, he used the stars to guide him, but he could also use a compass. He had to navigate through storm clouds, fog, and ice. He had to stay awake for the entire 33 1/2 hour flight because he was the only one on board. Charles finally arrived in Paris. He was the first pilot to fly from New York to Paris nonstop.

The Spirit of St. Louis was explicitly built for transatlantic flights. To hold 425 gallons of fuel it was longer than the average plane. Lindbergh designed it with a single-engine. He was aware that having only one engine was risky, but he felt it gave him a better chance of success. The plane was designed to be as aerodynamic as possible to maximize fuel efficiency. Lindbergh couldn't stretch his legs for the entire 33 1/2 hour flight because the cockpit was so tiny!

Lindbergh rose to fame after completing the journey. People all over the world regarded him as a hero. President Calvin Coolidge awarded him the Distinguished Flying Cross, and a huge parade was held in New York City in his honor. He traveled the world to promote aviation. During his travels, he met his future wife, Anne. On May 27, 1929, they married.

Tragic events occurred in the Lindbergh family in 1932. The Lindberghs' one-year-old son was abducted from their Hopewell, New Jersey home. Unfortunately, the boy was discovered dead in the woods ten weeks later. Bruno Hauptmann was arrested for kidnapping after two years of investigation. In what newspapers dubbed the "Trial of the Century," he was found guilty.

When World War II broke out, Lindbergh was opposed to the US getting involved. However, following the events of Pearl Harbor, he went to work as an advisor for the United States Army. During the war, he flew around 50 combat missions and assisted in the testing of new planes.

Charles Lindbergh died of cancer on the Hawaiian island of Maui on August 26, 1974.

---

Remember that there may be some question-answer relationship (QAR) questions, so please keep that in mind when answering the questions below.

1. **Charles Lindbergh was born on _____ in _____.**
   a. February 4, 1902, Detroit, Michigan
   b. January 29, 1905, Minneapolis, Minnesota
   c. January 7, 1900, Lindberg, Germany

2. **Charles' mother was _____.**
   a. a doctor
   b. an aviator
   c. a schoolteacher

3. On May 20, 1927, Charles took off from New York aboard his plane, the _____.
   a. Spirit of St. Luke
   b. Spirit of St. Louis
   c. Spirit of St. Joseph

4. _____ were pilots that traveled the country performing stunts and giving people rides at air shows.
   a. Barnstormers
   b. Sports pilot
   c. Recreational pilot

5. Charles died in _____ at _____.
   a. August 24, 1976, Minneapolis, Minnesota
   b. August 26, 1974, Maui, Hawaii
   c. August 25 1975, Detroit Michigan

6. In 1924, Charles joined the _____ where he received formal training as a pilot.
   a. Army Signal Corps
   b. Army Air Service
   c. Army Aviation Branch

7. Charles Lindbergh was named the first ever _____ by Time Magazine in 1927.
   a. "Man of the Decade"
   b. "Man of the Year"
   c. "Man of the Half-Century"

8. In _____, Charles became a Brigadier General in the U.S. Air Force.
   a. 1954
   b. 1974
   c. 1929

9. When World War II began, Lindbergh flew around _____ during the war and helped to test out new planes.
   a. 50 combat missions
   b. 60 combat missions
   c. 40 combat missions

10. Charles was awarded the _____ by President Calvin Coolidge and a huge parade was held for him in New York City.
    a. Aerial Achievement Medal
    b. Air Force Achievement Medal
    c. Distinguished Flying Cross

11. Charles contributed to the development of _____.
    a. an air pump
    b. an artificial heart pump
    c. a water pump

12. Charles was one of the best-known figures in aeronautical history, remembered for the first nonstop solo flight across the Atlantic Ocean, from New York City to _____, on May 20–21, 1927.
    a. United Kingdom
    b. Italy
    c. Paris

Charles Augustus Lindbergh was an aviator, military officer, author, inventor, and activist from the United States. At the age of 25, he rose from obscurity as a US Air Mail pilot to instant worldwide fame when he won the Orteig Prize for making the first nonstop flight from New York City to Paris on May 20–21, 1927.

# 5th Grade Geography Quiz: Fiji

Score: _____

Date: _____

Fiji is a country made up of about 300 islands in the South Pacific Ocean. Only about 100 of the islands are inhabited. Suva, the capital, is located on Viti Levu Island.

Fiji's islands cover an area of approximately 1 million square miles (3 million square kilometers). The coasts of the two largest islands, Viti Levu and Vanua Levu, are dominated by mountains. Many of the islands are surrounded by coral reefs. Fiji has a hot, wet season and a cooler, drier season every year.

On the eastern sides of the larger islands, there are dense tropical forests and mangrove swamps. The western sides are covered in dry grasslands. Most Fiji's animals, such as pigs, dogs, cattle, and horses, are domesticated or owned by humans. Snakes and rats on the islands are preyed upon by wild mongooses.

Native Fijians account for roughly half of the population. They are primarily Christian. The majority of the rest of the population's ancestors came from India. The majority of Indians are Hindus, but some are Muslims. The official languages are English, Fijian, and Hindustani. Cities house slightly more than half of the population, primarily along the coasts.

Tourism is the primary economic activity in Fiji. Clothing, sugar, fish, and gold are also produced in Fiji. Other important resources include wood and mineral water. Agriculture, on the other hand, employs the most people. Sugarcane, coconuts, taro, cassava, rice, bananas, and sweet potatoes are the main crops in Fiji.

The first settlers in Fiji arrived at least 3,500 years ago from other Pacific islands. In the late 1700s, the British explored the islands. In 1874, the United Kingdom established Fiji as a colony. Thousands of Indians were brought to work on the British sugar estates.

Fiji became independent in 1970. Tensions between native Fijians and Indians have resulted in several government changes since then.

---

Remember that there may be some question-answer relationship (QAR) questions, so please keep that in mind when answering the questions below.

1. **Fiji, officially the Republic of Fiji, is an island country in the _____.**
   a. Arctic Ocean
   b. North Pacific Ocean
   c. South Pacific Ocean

2. **Bula, which means _____ in Fijian, is the first word you'll need to learn because you'll hear it everywhere.**
   a. Welcome
   b. Good day
   c. Hello

3. **What is the capital and largest city of Fiji?**
   a. Lautoka
   b. Nadi
   c. Suva

4. **What is the climate in Fiji?**
   a. Dry
   b. Tropical marine
   c. Temperate continental

5. **____, ____, and _____ are the official languages of Fiji.**
   a. English, Fijian, and Samoan
   b. Fijian, Māori, and Rotuman
   c. English, Fijian, and Hindustan

6. **The native Fijians are mostly _____ and the Indo-Fijians are mostly Hindu.**
   a. Christians
   b. Catholics
   c. Buddhist

7. The traditional cooking method in Fiji is called _____.
   a. ahima'a
   b. uma
   c. lovo

8. After 96 years of British rule, Fiji became independent in _____ but remained part of the British Commonwealth.
   a. May 10, 1977
   b. October 10, 1970
   c. June 11, 1970

9. The original settlers of Fiji were _____ and _____ peoples who have lived on the islands for thousands of years.
   a. Austronesian, Micronesian
   b. Polynesian, Melanesian
   c. Polynesian and Micronesian

10. _____ is a Fijian military leader who led a 2006 coup that resulted in his becoming acting president (2006–07) and later acting prime minister (2007–14) of Fiji.
    a. Ratu Epeli Nailatikau
    b. Frank Bainimarama
    c. Laisenia Qarase

11. Fiji was ruled by one military coup after another until a democratic election was held in _____.
    a. September of 2014
    b. October of 2014
    c. November of 2014

12. What are Fiji's two largest islands?
    a. Kadavu & Mamanuca
    b. Viti Levu & Vanua Levu
    c. Rotuma & Lomaiviti

13. What country owns Fiji?
    a. USA
    b. British
    c. Italy

14. What is one of the languages do people mostly speak in Fiji?
    a. Fijian
    b. Portuguese
    c. Chinese

15. Who came to Fiji first?
    a. Duchess explorer Eden Thomas
    b. Dutch explorer Abel Janszoon Tasman
    c. John J Walker of Fiji

16. Where did the nickname "Fiji" come from?
    a. From the government
    b. From the people of Fiji
    c. From the Phi Gams at New York University

17. What is Fiji known for?
    a. grassland and hurricanes
    b. landfills
    c. tropical islands

18. What is the capital of Fiji?
    a. Suva
    b. Silva
    c. Selmer

# 5th Grade Geography: Lebanon

Score:_____

Date:_____

Lebanon's land was settled thousands of years ago. The city of Byblos is one of the world's oldest continuously inhabited cities. The Phoenician Empire arose from the land of Lebanon around 1500 BC. They were seafaring people with a culture that thrived and spread throughout the Mediterranean. The Phoenicians ruled until around 300 BC, when the Persian Empire led by Cyrus the Great conquered the land. Tyre was the most well-known Phoenician city. In 332 BC, Alexander the Great burned Tyre. Over time, the land of Lebanon would be ruled by several empires, including the Romans, Arabs, and, finally, the Ottoman Empire. When the Ottoman Empire fell apart following World War I, France seized control of Lebanon. Lebanon gained independence from France in 1943. Lebanon has been involved in wars with Israel as well as internal civil wars since its independence.

Lebanon is a small Middle Eastern country bordered by Syria and Israel. People first established villages in Lebanon over 7,000 years ago. The country has been ravaged by wars, the majority of which have been religious in nature. Following Christ's death, a monk named Maron established a monastery in the hills of Lebanon to avoid persecution by Roman officials. He and the other monks spread Christianity throughout Lebanon and much of the Middle East from here. When Muslim Arabs invaded Lebanon, they converted the majority of the population to Islam.

In the 11th century, the Pope dispatched knights from Europe to re-convert the Middle East to Christianity, resulting in more religious wars. In the late twentieth century, Christian and Muslim factions in Lebanon fought a civil war. Today, the country is still plagued by violence due to the civil war in Syria, which occasionally spills over into Lebanon.

The climate in Lebanon is Mediterranean. Summers are hot and dry, while winters are cool and wet. Mountains, hills, coastal plains, and deserts can all be found in the country.

---

Remember that there may be some question-answer relationship (QAR) questions, so please keep that in mind when answering the questions below.

1. Lebanon is a country in the _____, on the Mediterranean Sea.
   a. Middle East
   b. Western Europe
   c. Africa

2. Lebanon has _____ rivers all of which are non-navigable.
   a. 16
   b. 18
   c. 17

3. What is the capital city of Lebanon?
   a. Tyre
   b. Sidon
   c. Beirut

4. Lebanon has a moderate _____.
   a. Mediterranean climate
   b. Continental climate
   c. Temperate climate

5. When the Ottoman Empire collapsed after World War I, which country took control of Lebanon?
   a. France
   b. Britain
   c. Russia

6. When did Lebanon become a sovereign under the authority of the Free French government?
   a. November 26, 1943
   b. September 1, 1926
   c. May 25, 1926

7. What is the national symbol in Lebanon?
   a. Maple tree
   b. Pine tree
   c. Cedar tree

8. Lebanon is bordered by _____ to the north and east, _____ to the south, and the Mediterranean Sea to the west.
   a. Israel, France
   b. Japan, Korea
   c. Syria, Israel

9. Lebanon is divided into how many governorates?
    a. 7
    b. 8
    c. 6

10. The Cedar Revolution occurred in 2005, following the assassination of Lebanese Prime Minister _____ in a car bomb explosion.
    a. Fakhr-al-Din II
    b. Rafik Hariri
    c. Jabal Amel

11. The city of _____ is one of the oldest continuously inhabited cities in the world.
    a. Byblos
    b. Baalbek
    c. Beirut

12. Lebanon is divided into how many districts?
    a. 24
    b. 25
    c. 22

13. Lebanon's capital and largest city is _____.
    a. Brunitz
    b. Beirut
    c. Whales

14. Lebanon was conquered by the _____ Empire in the 16th century
    a. Ottoman
    b. Overmann
    c. US troops

15. Lebanon is a _____ country.
    a. strong
    b. developing
    c. newly built

16. Lebanon gained a measure of independence while France was occupied by _____.
    a. China
    b. Maine
    c. Germany

17. Lebanon supported neighboring Arab countries in a war against _____.
    a. Israel
    b. Africa
    c. United States

18. How old is Lebanon?
    a. nearly 200 years of history
    b. nearly 5,000 years of history
    c. nearly 1 million years of history

# 5th Grade Geography: Mountain Range

Score: _____

Date: _____

A mountain range is a collection of connected mountains that often form a long line of mountains. Large mountain ranges are frequently composed of smaller mountain ranges known as subranges. The Smokey Mountain Range, for example, is a section of the Appalachian Mountain Range. It is a subdivision of the Appalachian Mountains.

The Himalayas are the world's highest mountain range, while the Andes are the world's longest.

The Himalayas span 1,491 miles across a large portion of central Asia. They travel from Afghanistan and Pakistan to Bhutan via India, Nepal, and China. In addition to the Himalayas, the Karakoram and Hindu Kush mountain ranges are included.

The Himalayas are renowned for their lofty peaks. The Himalayas are home to most of the world's tallest mountains, including the world's two tallest peaks, Mount Everest at 29,035 feet and K2 at 28,251 feet.

The Himalayas have played a significant role in Asia's history. Many religions, including Buddhism and Hinduism, regard Tibet's mountains and high peaks as sacred.

The Andes Mountains, approximately 4,300 miles in length, is the world's longest mountain range. The Andes Mountains run north to south across a large portion of South America, passing through Argentina, Chile, Peru, Bolivia, Venezuela, Colombia, and Ecuador. Mount Aconcagua, at 22,841 feet, is the Andes' tallest peak. The Andes played a critical role in South America's history. Machu Picchu, the Inca's famous ancient city, was built high in the Andes.

The Alps are a significant mountain range that runs through central Europe. They traverse through several nations in Europe, including France, Germany, Switzerland, Italy, Austria, and Slovenia. Mont Blanc, at 15,782 feet, is the highest summit in the Alps, located on the French-Italian boundary.

Over time, the Alps cemented their position in history. Perhaps the most famous instance occurred during the Punic Wars when Hannibal of Carthage crossed the Alps to attack Rome.

The Rocky Mountains span western North America from north to south. They connect Canada and the United States of America's state of New Mexico. Mount Elbert, at 14,440 feet, is the tallest peak in the Rockies.

The Sierra Nevada Mountain Range runs parallel to the Rockies in the United States but further west. Beautiful national parks, like Yosemite and Kings Canyon, are located here. Mount Whitney, at 14,505 feet, is the tallest mountain in the contiguous United States.

On the eastern coast of the United States, the Appalachian Mountains stretch parallel to the Atlantic Ocean.

In western Russia, the Ural Mountains run north to south. The eastern edge of these mountains is frequently seen as the dividing line or border between Europe and Asia.

The Pyrenees, Tian Shan, Transantarctic Mountains, Atlas, and the Carpathians are also significant world mountain ranges.

---

Remember that there may be some question-answer relationship (QAR) questions, so please keep that in mind when answering the questions below.

1. A _____ includes geological features that are in the same region as a mountain range.
   a. mountain passes
   b. mountain chain
   c. mountain system

2. _____ are smaller mountain ranges that can be found within larger mountain ranges.
   a. Hill ranges
   b. Subranges
   c. Micro ranges

3. **The world's tallest mountain ranges form when pieces of the Earth's crust, known as _____, collide.**
   a. core
   b. mantle
   c. plates

4. **The tallest mountain range in the world is the _____ and the longest is the _____.**
   a. Himalayas, Andes
   b. Andes, Mt. Vinson
   c. Mt. Everest, Manaslu

5. **Mountain ranges usually include highlands or _____.**
   a. mountain passes and valleys
   b. valleys and rifts
   c. mountain peaks and edges

6. **The Andes Mountains are the world's longest mountain range, stretching approximately _____.**
   a. 4,300 miles
   b. 5,000 miles
   c. 2,000 miles

7. **_____ is a scientific theory that explains how major landforms are created as a result of Earth's subterranean movements.**
   a. Erosion
   b. Plate tectonics
   c. Sedimentation

8. **The Himalayas run 1,491 miles across much of _____.**
   a. Central Europe
   b. South America
   c. Central Asia

9. **What is the highest peak in the Rocky Mountain Range that is 14,440 feet tall?**
   a. Mt. Everest
   b. Mt. Elbert
   c. Mt. Mayon

10. **The majority of geologically young mountain ranges on Earth's land surface are found in either the _____ or the _____.**
    a. Alpide belt, Oceanic Ridge belt
    b. Pacific Ring of Fire, Alpide Belt
    c. Oceanic Ridge belt, Circum-Pacific Seismic Belt

11. **The _____ runs somewhat parallel to the Rockies, but further west in the United States.**
    a. Sierra Nevada Mountain Range
    b. Appalachian
    c. Himalayas

12. **Mountains often serve as _____ that define the natural borders of countries.**
    a. enclosure
    b. geographic features
    c. barriers

# 5th Grade Science: Endangered Animals

Score: _____

Date: _____

Endangered animals are those that are on the verge of extinction. This means there will be no more of these animals on the planet. When very few of an animal's species are left alive, it is considered endangered or "threatened."

Some animals are in greater danger than others. Scientists assign different names to different levels of risk to keep track of how close a species is to become extinct. These are the names, from most threatened to least threaten, of the following animals:

1) critically endangered 2) endangered 3) vulnerable

Some animals can only be found in zoos (for example, in a zoo). These animals are referred to as "extinct in the wild."

Many countries around the world have legislation in place to protect endangered species. Killing or injuring an endangered or protected animal is frequently a crime. Several laws in the United States protect endangered animals. These laws are part of the Endangered Species Act, which President Nixon signed into law in 1973. These laws aid in the protection of animals and their habitats. They also include Recovery Plans, which are programs that help in the recovery of animals. The United States Fish and Wildlife Service and the National Oceanic and Atmospheric Administration are the primary agencies enforcing the laws and protecting the animals.

There are also wildlife or nature preserves all over the world. These are large swaths of land where animals and their habitats are safeguarded. On the grounds, development is severely restricted or prohibited entirely. Hunting is also banned or prohibited. Critically endangered animals are frequently protected by capturing some of them and breeding them in captivity. This allows scientists to keep the species alive while also studying the animals.

Many species have gone extinct throughout history. This is a normal part of the process. Species may become extinct due to climate change (e.g., the ice age), competition with other species, a reduced food supply, or a combination of all of these factors. The majority of natural extinctions are isolated events that occur over a relatively long period. Some, on the other hand, are significant events that can cause mass extinctions and happen quickly. The most well-known of these was the extinction of the dinosaurs, which may have been caused by a large meteorite striking the Earth.

Many species have been hunted to extinction or have become critically endangered. The American bison is one example of this. Before the arrival of the Europeans, the Great Plains of North America were home to millions of bison. Hunting was so intense that by the time the animals were protected, only a few hundred remained. They have, thankfully, survived on farms and ranches and are no longer endangered.

Species that only exist on islands are also easily hunted to extinction. Even the arrival of a small tribe can be enough to wipe out an island species.

Aside from food, animals are frequently hunted for specific body parts such as fur, feathers, or horns. Because these animals are sometimes the top predators, they do not have a large population, to begin with. These species can be hunted to extinction in a short period.

The elephant was heavily hunted in Africa for its valuable ivory horns. The population shrank from millions to a few hundred thousand people. The elephant is now protected, but its population is still declining in some areas due to poachers.

Another example is the Chinese tiger. Tigers were nearly hunted to extinction for their valuable fur and their bones, which were traditionally used in medicine. It is still listed as an endangered species today.

One of the most severe threats to animals today is habitat loss. This is due to the expansion of humans, mainly through agriculture. Natural habitats are being destroyed as vast areas of land are cultivated to grow food. This can disrupt many of the life cycles required for organisms to survive and biomes to thrive.

Pollution caused by humans can also lead to the extinction of a species. This is particularly true in freshwater biomes like rivers and lakes. Sewage and industrial plant runoff can contaminate the water. Other species may perish when one species is harmed, resulting in a chain reaction that destroys the ecosystem's balance.

---

Remember that there may be some question-answer relationship (QAR) questions, so please keep that in mind when answering the questions below.

1. In 1973, an international treaty known as _____ was adopted as a far-reaching wildlife conservation measure.
    a. International Union for Conservation of Nature (IUCN)
    b. Convention on International Trade in Endangered Species of Wild Fauna and Flora (CITES)
    c. Wildlife (Protection) Act

2. _____ programs can help protect endangered species.
    a. Preservation
    b. Conservation
    c. Restoration

3. The Endangered Species Act was signed into law by _____ in 1973.
    a. John Dingell (D-Mich.)
    b. Richard Nixon
    c. Richard Pallardy

4. What percent of threatened species are at risk because of human activities alone?
    a. Below 50 %
    b. Almost 50 %
    c. Roughly 99 %

5. These animals are listed as critically endangered because they are primarily threatened by hunters who kill them for their horns.
    a. Black rhinoceros
    b. Oryx
    c. Antelope

6. Who wrote the Endangered Species Act and argued that "only natural extinction is part of natural order?"
    a. Julian Huxley
    b. Richard Nixon
    c. John Dingell (D-Mich.)

7. Species that only exist in captivity (for example in a zoo), are called _____.
    a. extinct in the wild
    b. extinct species
    c. critically endangered species

8. It is defined as any species that is at risk of extinction because of a sudden, rapid decrease in its population or a loss of its critical habitat.
    a. Endangered Animals
    b. Exotic Species
    c. Distinct Species

9. It is a law that protects endangered animals by taking into account any destruction to a species' habitat, whether it has been over-consumed, any disease or predation that threatens it, and whether any other man-made factors put it in danger.
    a. The Republic Act of 1947
    b. The United States' Endangered Species Act of 1973
    c. The Wildlife (Protection) Act of 1972

10. 10. By the early 21st century, it could be said that _____ are the greatest threat to biodiversity.
    a. human beings (Homo sapiens)
    b. wild animals
    c. exotic plants

11. Choose the correct order of the level of risk, starting with the most threatened animal and working your way down to the least threatened.
    a. Critically endangered, Endangered, Vulnerable
    b. b.Endangered, Critically Endangered, Vulnerable
    c. a.Critically endangered, Vulnerable, Endangered

12. The most pervasive threat to species in the wild is:
    a. Unsustainable hunting
    b. Habitat loss and habitat degradation
    c. Disease

# 5th Grade Science: Food Chain and Food Web

Score: _____

Date: _____

In the wild, the food chain describes who eats whom. Every living thing, from single-celled algae to massive blue whales, requires food to survive. Each food chain represents a potential path for energy and nutrients to travel through the ecosystem.

Grass, for example, generates its food from sunlight. A rabbit is eating the grass. A fox devours the rabbit. When a fox dies, bacteria decompose its body and return it to the soil, providing nutrients to plants such as grass. To survive, every living plant and animal requires energy. Plants get their energy from the soil, water, and the sun. Plants and other animals provide energy to animals.

Plants and animals in an ecosystem rely on one another to survive. Scientists may use a food chain or a food web to describe this dependence.

Of course, many different animals consume grass, and rabbits can consume plants other than grass. Foxes, in turn, can consume a wide range of animals and plants. Each of these living things has the potential to be a part of multiple food chains. A food web is made up of all of the interconnected and overlapping food chains in an ecosystem.

Each link in the food chain has a name to help describe it. The names are determined mainly by what the organism eats and how it contributes to its energy.

Producers - Plants are creators. This is because they generate energy for the ecosystem. They do this because photosynthesis absorbs energy from the sun. They require water and nutrients from the soil as well, but plants are the only source of new energy.

Consumers - Consumers include animals. This is since they do not generate energy; instead, they consume it. Primary consumers, also known as herbivores, are animals that eat plants. Secondary consumers or carnivores are animals that eat other animals. A carnivore is referred to as a tertiary consumer when it consumes another carnivore. Some animals perform both functions, eating both plants and animals. They are known as omnivores.

All of the energy produced in the food chain is produced by producers or plants, who convert sunlight into energy through photosynthesis. The rest of the food chain merely consumes energy. As a result, as you move up the food chain, less and less energy is available. As a result, as you move up the food chain, there are fewer and fewer organisms.

Many different food chains that make up a food web can be found in various habitats and ecosystems.

Single-celled organisms known as phytoplankton provide food for tiny shrimp known as krill in one marine food chain. Krill are the primary food source for blue whales, which are classified as being on the third trophic level.

A grasshopper may consume grass, a producer, in a grassland ecosystem. The grasshopper may be eaten by a rat, which a snake then eats. Finally, an apex predator, a hawk, swoops down and snatches up the snake.

The autotroph in a pond could be algae. A mosquito larva consumes the algae, and then a dragonfly larva consumes the young mosquito. The dragonfly larva is eaten by a fish, which then becomes a tasty meal for a raccoon.

---

Remember that there may be some question-answer relationship (QAR) questions, so please keep that in mind when answering the questions below.

1. **In ecology, it is the sequence of transfers of matter and energy in the form of food from organism to organism.**
   a. Food Sequencing
   b. Food Transport
   c. Food Chain

2. **_____ can increase the total food supply by cutting out one step in the food chain.**
   a. Birds
   b. Animals
   c. People

3. **Plants, which convert solar energy to food by photosynthesis, are the _____.**
   a. secondary food source
   b. tertiary food source
   c. primary food source

4. **_____ help us understand how changes to ecosystems affect many different species, both directly and indirectly.**
   a. Food Transport
   b. Food Chain
   c. Food Web

5. _____ eat decaying matter and are the ones who help put nutrients back into the soil for plants to eat.
   a. Decomposers
   b. Consumers
   c. Producers

6. _____ are producers because they produce energy for the ecosystem.
   a. Animals
   b. Decomposers
   c. Plants

7. Each organism in an ecosystem occupies a specific _____ in the food chain or web.
   a. trophic level
   b. space
   c. place

8. What do you call an organism that eats both plants and animals?
   a. Omnivores
   b. Herbivores
   c. Carnivores

9. Carnivore is from the Latin word that means _____.
   a. "flesh devourers"
   b. "eats both plants and animals"
   c. "plant eaters"

10. A food web is all of the interactions between the species within a community that involve the transfer of energy through _____.
    a. consumption
    b. reservation
    c. adaptation

11. Why are animals considered consumers?
    a. because they produce energy for the ecosystem
    b. because they don't produce energy, they just use it up
    c. because they only produce energy for themselves

12. How do plants turn sunlight energy into chemical energy?
    a. through the process of photosynthesis
    b. through the process of adaptation
    c. through the process of cancelation

13. Grass produces its own food from_____,
    a. animals
    b. sunlight
    c. soil

14. Each of these living things can be a part of _____ food chains.
    a. zero
    b. multiple
    c. only one

15. When an animal dies, _____ breaks down its body.
    a. bacteria
    b. grass
    c. sunlight

# 5th Grade Science: Temperate Forest Biome

Score: _____

Date: _____

There are many trees in all forests, but there are different types of forests. They are frequently referred to as different biomes. One of the most noticeable differences is where they are in relation to the equator and the poles. Forest biomes are classified into three types: rainforest, temperate forest, and taiga. Rainforests are found near the equator in the tropics. Taiga forests are found in the far north. Temperate rainforests are found in the middle.

**Temperature** - Temperate means "in moderation" or "not to extremes." Temperate refers to the temperature in this context. The temperate forest never gets extremely hot (as in the rainforest) or extremely cold (as in the Taiga). The temperature ranges between -20 and 90 degrees Fahrenheit.

**Four distinct seasons** - Winter, spring, summer, and fall are the four distinct seasons. Each season lasts roughly the same amount of time. Plants have a long growing season with only a three-month winter.

**Lots of rain** - Throughout the year, there is a lot of rain, usually between 30 and 60 inches. Fertile soil - Rotted leaves and other decaying matter create a rich, deep soil that allows trees to grow strong roots.

Temperate forests come in a variety of forms. Here are a few examples:

Coniferous forests are dominated by conifer trees such as cypress, cedar, redwood, fir, juniper, and pine. These trees have cones instead of flowers and grow needles instead of leaves.

Broad-leafed forests are made up of broad-leafed trees like oak, maple, elm, walnut, chestnut, and hickory. The leaves on these trees are large and change color in the fall.

Mixed coniferous and broad-leaved forests - These forests contain a mixture of conifers and broad-leaved trees.

Major temperate forests can be found all over the world, including:

Eastern North America
Southeast Australia
New Zealand
Eastern China
Europe
Japan

The plants in the forests grow in layers. The canopy is the top layer, which is made up of fully grown trees. Throughout the year, these trees form an umbrella, providing shade for the layers below. The understory refers to the middle layer. Smaller trees, saplings, and shrubs make up the understory. The forest floor, which is made up of wildflowers, herbs, ferns, mushrooms, and mosses, is the lowest layer.

The plants that grow here share some characteristics.

They shed their leaves - Many of the trees that grow here are deciduous, which means they shed their leaves in the winter. There are a few evergreen trees that keep their leaves throughout the winter.

Sap - sap is used by many trees to help them survive the winter. It keeps their roots from freezing and is then used as energy to start growing again in the spring.

Animals that live here include black bears, mountain lions, deer, fox, squirrels, skunks, rabbits, porcupines, timber wolves, and a variety of birds. Mountain lions and hawks, for example, are predators. Many animals, such as squirrels and turkeys, rely on the nuts from the many trees to survive.

Each animal species has adapted to survive the winter.

Stay active - Some animals remain active throughout the winter. There are rabbits, squirrels, foxes, and deer, all of which are active.

Some are simply good at finding food, whereas others, such as squirrels, store and hide food in the fall so that they can eat it during the winter.

Migrate - Some animals, such as birds, migrate to warmer areas for the winter and then return home in the spring.

Hibernate - During the winter, some animals hibernate or rest. They basically sleep all winter and survive on fat stored in their bodies.

Many insects die and lay eggs because they cannot survive the winter, but they lay eggs that can. In the spring, their eggs will hatch.

---

Remember that there may be some question-answer relationship (QAR) questions, so please keep that in mind when answering the questions below.

1. _____ are found in Northern Hemisphere regions with moist, warm summers and cold winters, primarily in eastern North America, eastern Asia, and western Europe.
    a. Wild forests
    b. Rainforests
    c. Deciduous forests

2. How many types of forest biomes are there?
    a. 2
    b. 3
    c. 4

3. **Temperate forests emerged during the period of global cooling that began at the beginning of the _____.**
    a. Medieval Era
    b. Paleozoic Era
    c. Cenozoic Era

4. **Major temperate forests are located in the following areas, except for:**
    a. Japan
    b. Korea
    c. Eastern China

5. What makes a forest a temperate forest?
    a. Temperature, Two seasons, Tropics, and Clay soil.
    b. Temperature, Climate, Wet season, and Loam soil.
    c. Temperature, Four seasons, Lots of rain, and Fertile soil.

6. **The three main types of forest biomes are: the rainforest, the temperate forest, and the _____.**
    a. Taiga
    b. Broad-leafed
    c. Coniferous

7. Many trees rely on _____ to get through the winter.
    a. temperature
    b. sap
    c. rain

8. **Temperate forests are usually classified into two main groups, and these are: _____ and _____.**
    a. Indigenous, Evergreen
    b. Deciduous, Evergreen
    c. Coniferous, Deciduous

9. Deciduous is a Latin word that means _____.
    a. "to subside"
    b. "to rise up"
    c. "to fall off"

10. **Certain trees in a temperate forest can grow up to how many feet?**
    a. 50 feet tall
    b. 90 feet tall
    c. 100 feet tall

11. _____ forests are made up mostly of conifer trees such as cypress, cedar, redwood, fir, juniper, and pine trees.
    a. Coniferous
    b. Broad-leafed
    c. Mixed coniferous and broad-leafed

12. **The animals that live in temperate forests have _____ that allow them to _____ in different kinds of weather.**
    a. adaptations, survive
    b. conformity, thrive
    c. compatibility, survive

# 5th Grade Art: J. M. W. Turner
## Reading Comprehension

Score: _____

Date: _____

Joseph Mallord William Turner, also known as William Turner, was an English Romantic painter, printmaker, and watercolorist. He is well-known for his expressive colorizations, imaginative landscapes, and turbulent, often violent sea paintings.

On April 23, 1775, J. M. W. Turner was born above his father's barbershop in London, England. When Joseph was a child, he began to draw pictures. He enjoyed drawing outside scenes, particularly buildings. His father's shop sold some of his drawings.

He began attending the Royal Academy of Art in London when he was fourteen years old. He kept sketching and painting with watercolors. Many of his sketches were published in magazines. While he mostly drew buildings and architecture, he also began to draw some seascapes.

In 1796, Turner completed his first oil painting. Fishermen at Sea was the title. Turner gained a national reputation as a talented artist as a result of the painting's critical acclaim. Many people compared his work to that of other well-known painters.

Turner was captivated by the power of God in natural scenes, particularly the ocean and the sun. He would make numerous sketches in numbered notebooks, which he would then reference when painting in his studio. He frequently included people in his paintings, but they were small and insignificant compared to the power of nature around them.

Turner's work evolved, with less emphasis on detail and more emphasis on the energy of the natural phenomenon he was painting, such as the sea, a storm, a fire, or the sun. The paintings' objects became less recognizable.

The painting Rain, Steam, and Speed is an example of this. Light and mist are used to power the train engine as it moves down the track in this landscape of a locomotive crossing a bridge. The focus is on the color and changing light as the train passes through the landscape.

Many of Turner's later works are reminiscent of the Impressionist style of painting that would emerge in France in the coming years. Turner's work undoubtedly influenced artists like Monet, Degas, and Renoir.

Many art historians regard J. M. W. Turner as the most incredible landscape painter of all time. His artwork had a significant influence on many artists who came after him, including many impressionists.

1. Turner's later works are reminiscent of the _____ style of painting.
    a. Impressionist
    b. Watercolor

2. In 1796, Turner completed his first _____ painting.
    a. colored
    b. oil

3. Turner began attending the _____ of Art in London.
    a. Royal State University
    b. Royal Academy

4. Turner was born above his father's _____.
    a. mechanic shop
    b. barbershop

5. J. M. W. Turner was an English Romantic painter, _____, and watercolorist.
    a. teacher
    b. printmaker

6. Turner frequently included _____ in his painting.
    a. animals
    b. people

# 5th Grade Art: Abstract Art
## Reading Comprehension

In the United States, there was an Abstract Art movement. Abstract art has no subject in its purest form. It consists solely of lines, shapes, and colors. Abstract Expressionism is the name given to the Abstract Art movement because, despite the lack of a subject, the art attempts to convey some emotion.

Following World War II, the Abstract Expressionism movement began in the 1940s in New York City. However, some Expressionists, particularly Wassily Kandinsky, painted the first true Abstract Art in the early 1900s.

The main feature of abstract art is that it lacks a recognizable subject. Some Abstract Artists had theories about the emotions elicited by different colors and shapes. They meticulously planned their seemingly random paintings. Other Abstract Artists painted with emotion and randomness in the hope of capturing their feelings and subconscious thoughts on canvas.

Mondrian's paintings are filled with precision and geometric shapes. In this painting, he uses straight black lines, white spaces, and primary colors to create a sense of balance. He painted several other pictures in the same style.

Mark Rothko created many large color blocks in his paintings. There was usually a border, and the edges of the blocks were blurred together, as in this painting. Rothko never explained what the painting was supposed to mean. He left it up to the viewer to make their interpretations. As simple as it appears here, this painting sold for more than $72 million in 2007.

Jackson Pollock developed his distinct painting style. He would splatter and dribble paint directly from the can onto the canvas. This art form was later dubbed "Action Painting." Yellow and brown paint is drizzled in this painting to create an exciting nest of colors and textures. The painting was sold for a whopping $140 million in 2006.

1. Who splatters and dribbles paint directly from the can onto the canvas?
    a. Mark Rothko
    b. Jackson Pollock

2. Abstract Art consists solely of lines, ___, and colors.
    a. pictures
    b. shapes

3. Abstract Expressionism movement began in the 1940s in _____.
    a. Washington
    b. New York City

4. _____ created many large color blocks in his paintings.
    a. Mark Rothko
    b. John Mondrian

5. The main feature of abstract art is that it lacks a _____ subject.
    a. recognizable
    b. colorful

6. _____ paintings are filled with precision and geometric shapes.
    a. Mondrian's
    b. Rothko

7. The Abstract Expressionism movement began in the _____.
    a. The 1940s
    b. The 1840s

8. Based on what you read, what do you think is the main idea of abstract art?
    a. Not to tell a story, but to encourage involvement and imagination.
    b. Tell a true story and show emotions.

9. Who painted the first true Abstract Art in the early 1900s?
    a. Walter Kondiskny
    b. Wassily Kandinsky

10. Some abstract artists painted with emotion and _____.
    a. randomness
    b. black lines and dots

# 5th Grade Music: The Piano
## Reading Comprehension

Bartolomeo Cristofori was the first to successfully develop a hammer-action keyboard instrument and hence deserves to be regarded as the creator of the piano.

Cristofori was dissatisfied with musicians' lack of control over the harpsichord's loudness level. Around 1700, he is credited for replacing the plucking mechanism with a hammer and thus creating the modern piano. Initially, the instrument was dubbed "clavicembalo con piano e forte" (literally, a harpsichord that can play soft and loud noises). This was later abbreviated to the now-common term "piano."

The piano possesses the characteristics of both a string and percussion instrument. A hammer strikes a string inside the piano (much like a percussion instrument). The piano's sounds and notes are produced by the vibration of these strings (like a string instrument).

The piano is commonly referred to as a keyboard instrument. This is because it is performed similarly to several other keyboard instruments, including the organ, harpsichord, electronic keyboards, and synthesizers.

The organ was the first keyboard instrument, dating back to the third century. However, the organ did not begin to use keys until much later. The harpsichord was invented in the 14th century and quickly gained popularity throughout Europe. The harpsichord plucked a string and resembled modern pianos in appearance. However, plucking the string did not allow for the playing of various volumes and expressions.

The term piano is derived from the Italian phrase pianoforte, which translates as "loud and soft." This is because you may now adjust the volume of notes played on the keyboard.

The grand piano and the upright piano are the two primary types of pianos.

Grand piano - a grand piano's strings and primary frame are horizontal. This enables longer strings and also aids in the piano's mechanics. However, grand pianos can consume a significant amount of room.

Upright piano - This piano style is more compact, making it ideal for use in a home. The strings and mainframe are arranged vertically.

Additionally, there are electronic pianos. While the keyboard and playing technique is typically identical to a standard piano, the sound is frequently quite different.

1. This piano style is more compact, making it ideal for use in a home.
    a. Upright piano
    b. Downright piano

2. A ____ strings and primary frame are horizontal.
    a. organ piano's
    b. grand piano's

3. The term piano is derived from the_____phrase pianoforte.
    a. English
    b. Italian

4. The ____ was invented in the 14th century.
    a. pianiochord
    b. harpsichord

5. The piano is commonly referred to as a ____ instrument.
    a. singer
    b. keyboard

6. The organ and harpsichord are keyboard instruments.
    a. organ
    b. guitar

# 5th Grade Music: Jimi Hendrix
## Reading Comprehension

Score: _____

Date: _____

First, read the entire passage. After that, go back and fill in the blanks. You can skip the blanks you're unsure about and finish them later.

| guitar | odd | acoustic | mother | Animals |
| guitarist | stage | Seattle | rock | childhood |

Jimi Hendrix, a _____, singer, and songwriter, wowed audiences in the 1960s with his outrageous electric guitar skills and experimental sound.

Jimi Hendrix began playing guitar as a teenager and grew up to become a _____ legend known for his innovative electric guitar playing in the 1960s. His performance of "The Star-Spangled Banner" at Woodstock in 1969 was one of his most memorable. Hendrix died of drug-related complications in 1970, leaving his imprint on the world of rock music and remaining popular to this day.

On November 27, 1942, in _____, Washington, Hendrix was born Johnny Allen Hendrix (later changed by his father to James Marshall). He had a difficult _____, living in the care of relatives or acquaintances at times.

When Hendrix was born, his _____, Lucille, was only 17 years old. She had a rocky relationship with his father, Al, and eventually left the family after the couple had two more sons, Leon and Joseph. Hendrix only saw his mother on rare occasions before her death in 1958.

Music became a haven for Hendrix in many ways. He was a fan of blues and rock and roll and taught himself to play the _____ with the help of his father.

When Hendrix was 16, his father bought him his first _____ guitar, and the following year, his first electric guitar - a right-handed Supro Ozark that he had to play upside down because he was naturally left-handed. Soon after, he started performing with his band, the Rocking Kings. In 1959, he dropped out of high school and worked _____ jobs while pursuing his musical dreams.

In mid-1966, Hendrix met Chas Chandler, bassist for the British rock band the _____, who agreed to become Hendrix's manager. Chandler persuaded Hendrix to travel to London, where he formed the Jimi Hendrix Experience with bassist Noel Redding and drummer Mitch Mitchell.

While performing in England, Hendrix amassed a cult following among the country's rock royalty, with the Beatles, Rolling Stones, Who, and Eric Clapton all praising his work. According to one critic for the British music magazine Melody Maker, he "had great _____ presence" and appeared to be playing "with no hands at all" at times.

According to one journalist in the Berkeley Tribe, "Nobody could get more out of an electric guitar than Jimi Hendrix. He was the ultimate guitarist."

# A Community Garden Letter

Score: _____

Date: _____

First, read the questions. Then read the letter. Answer the questions by circling the correct letter.

Jill Kindle
780 Billings St.
Riverstide, MB
J9K 5G9

June 5, 2018

Dear Andrew,

Thank you for your letter asking about gardening plots in a community garden. There are two plots available in the Greendale Community Garden at 678 Warren Drive. The fee for the 10 x 10 plot is $45.00 per year and the 10 x 12 plot is $55.00 per year. The water is included. There are a couple gardening tools, but it is best to bring your own. I suggest you talk to Dawn Clover to get a key for the shed. You can write your name on your tools and keep them in the shed. Dawn is the coordinator and her phone number is 693-555-9009. Please send your cheque to:

    Greendale Community Garden
    c/o Dawn Clover
    789 Gibbons St.
    Riverstide, MB
    J8K 4G9

Thank you for your interest in the community garden program. We hope you have a fun time gardening this season.

Please let me know if you have any more questions.


Best regards,

Jill Kindle

Director of Community Gardens
City of Riverstide

# A Community Garden Letter Questions

Score: _____

Date: _____

1. Who sent this letter?
    a. Andrew Fitzgerald
    b. Jill Kindle
    c. Dawn Clover

2. Who is the letter for?
    a. Jill Kindle
    b. Dawn Clover
    c. Andrew Fitzgerald

3. How much is the 10 x 12 plot per year?
    a. $90.00
    b. $45.00
    c. $55.00

4. What is Dawn Clover's phone number?
    a. 693-555-9006
    b. 963-555-9669
    c. 693-555-9009

5. What job does Jill Kindle have?
    a. Community Garden Person
    b. Director of Community Gardens
    c. Garden Coordinator

6. What town or city is this community garden in?
    a. Gibbons
    b. Billings
    c. Riverstide

7. Where is the Greendale Community Garden?
    a. 678 Warren Drive
    b. 780 Billings St.
    c. 789 Gibbons St.

8. How many plots are available?
    a. 2
    b. 10
    c. 12

9. The water costs extra.
    a. True
    b. False

10. When was this letter written?
    a. June 5, 2018
    b. June 5, 2019
    c. June 9, 2015

# 5th Grade Reading Storytime: The Frog

Score: _____

Date: _____

First, read the entire passage. After that, go back and fill in the blanks. You can skip the blanks you're unsure about and finish them later.

| fountain | cried | companion | beautiful | ball |
| dinner | swimming | Frog | castle | door |

When wishing was a thing, there was a King whose daughters were all _____, but the youngest was so stunning that even the sun, which has seen so much, was taken aback whenever it shone in her face.

A large dark forest lay close to the King's _____, and a fountain was hidden beneath an old lime tree in the woods. When it was a hot day, the King's Child went out into the forest and sat by the cool fountain, and when she was bored, she took a golden ball, threw it up in the air, and caught it. And the ball was her favorite toy.

Now, one day, the King's Daughter's golden _____ fell onto the ground and rolled straight into the water rather than into the little hand she was holding up for it. The King's Daughter pursued it with her eyes, but it vanished, and the well was deep, so deep that the bottom could not be seen. She began to cry, and she screamed louder and louder, and she could not be consoled.

And as she sobbed, someone asked her, "What ails you, King's Daughter?" You weep so much that even a stone would feel sorry for you."

When she turned around to the side from which the voice had come, she saw a _____ sticking its thick, ugly head out of the water. "Ah! "Is it you, old water-splasher?" she asked, "I am weeping for my golden ball, which has fallen into the fountain."

"Be quiet and do not weep," the Frog replied, "I can help you." But what will you give me if I bring up your toy again?"

"Whatever you want, dear Frog," she said, "my clothes, my pearls, and jewels, even the golden crown I'm wearing."

"I don't care for your clothes, pearls, and jewels, or your golden crown," the Frog replied, "but if you will love me and let me be your _____ and playfellow, and sit by you at your little table, and eat off your little golden plate, and drink out of your little cup, and sleep in your little bed-if you promise me this, I will go down below and bring your golden ball up again."

"Oh, yes," she said, "I promise you everything you want if you just bring my ball back." "How the silly Frog does talk!" she thought. He lives in the water with the other frogs and croaks and can't be a human's companion!"

But, having received this promise, the Frog plunged his head into the water and sank. He quickly came _____ up with the ball in his mouth, and threw it on the grass. The King's Daughter was thrilled to see her pretty plaything again, and she quickly picked it up and ran away with it.

"Wait, wait," the Frog said. "Bring me along. I can't run as fast as you." But what good did it do him to scream his croak, croak, croak, croak, croak, croak! She ignored it and ran home, quickly forgetting the poor Frog, who was forced to return to his _____.

The next day, as she sat at the table with the King and all the courtiers, eating from her little golden plate, something crept up the marble staircase, splish splash, splish splash. When it reached the top, it knocked on the _____ and cried out:

"Youngest King's Daughter."

"Please open the door!"

She dashed outside to see who was there, but when she opened the door, the Frog was standing in front of it. Then she hurriedly slammed the door, sat down to _____ again, and was terrified.

"My Child, what are you so afraid of?" said the King, seeing her heart beating furiously. Is there a Giant outside looking to take you away?"

"Ah, no," she replied, "it's a disgusting Frog, not a Giant."

"What exactly does the Frog want from you?"

"Ah, dear Father, my golden ball fell into the water yesterday while I was sitting by the fountain in the forest, playing." Because I _____ so much, the Frog brought it out for me again. And because he insisted, I promised him he could be my companion, but I never imagined he'd be able to get out of the water! And now he's here, wanting to come in."

Meanwhile, it knocked a second time and cried:

"Youngest King's Daughter!"

Allow me to enter!

Don't you remember yesterday and everything you said to me, besides the cooling fountain's spray?

Youngest King's Daughter!

"Let me in!"

# 5th Grade Spelling Words

Score: _____

Date: _____

Write and circle the correct spelling for each word.

| | | A | B | C | D |
|---|---|---|---|---|---|
| 1. | _____ | grravity | grraviti | graviti | gravity |
| 2. | _____ | jewelri | jewellri | jewellry | jewelry |
| 3. | _____ | obstroct | obstruct | obsctruct | obsstruct |
| 4. | _____ | trompet | trrumpet | trumpet | trrompet |
| 5. | _____ | imigrant | imygrant | immygrant | immigrant |
| 6. | _____ | oxygen | oxygfn | oxyjen | oxyjtn |
| 7. | _____ | sensse | sence | sense | sensce |
| 8. | _____ | judje | juqje | judge | judne |
| 9. | _____ | altitode | alltitude | alltitode | altitude |
| 10. | _____ | December | Decemberr | Desember | Desemberr |
| 11. | _____ | tolerable | tolerible | tollerible | tollerable |
| 12. | _____ | acttive | actyve | acttyve | active |
| 13. | _____ | aware | awarre | awarra | awara |
| 14. | _____ | trryple | tryple | trriple | triple |
| 15. | _____ | exselent | excelent | exsellent | excellent |
| 16. | _____ | adaptible | adapttible | adaptable | adapttable |
| 17. | _____ | Ausstralia | Ausstralai | Australai | Australia |
| 18. | _____ | syngle | singlle | single | synglle |
| 19. | _____ | launch | luanch | laonch | loanch |
| 20. | _____ | smyled | smilled | smiled | smylled |
| 21. | _____ | finanse | finance | finense | finence |
| 22. | _____ | climb | cllymb | cllimb | clymb |
| 23. | _____ | introducsion | inttroduction | introduction | inttroducsion |
| 24. | _____ | Japanece | Japanese | Japanesse | Japanesce |
| 25. | _____ | specillize | specialize | specailize | specaillize |
| 26. | _____ | gulible | gullible | gulable | gullably |

# 5th Grade Spelling Words

Score: _____

Date: _____

Unscramble the spelling words below.

Tip: Unscramble the words you are sure about first.

| afraid | entire | absent | caught | lawyer | ancestor |
| adapt | subordinate | permissible | freight | naughty | captain |
| flavor | complaining | feast | interact | compliant | rounding |
| comic | route | insects | youth | menu | exactly |
| Saturn | scissors | | | | |

1. osssicrs     _ c _ _ _ o _ _

2. hgynatu     _ a _ g _ _ _

3. ifrgteh     _ r _ i _ _ _

4. aadrfi     _ f _ a _ _

5. seaft     _ e _ _ _

6. rtnsau     S _ t _ _ _

7. itureabdnos     _ _ _ _ r _ _ _ a t _

8. tetarnic     _ _ t _ _ _ c _

9. scensit     i _ _ _ _ _ s

10. ipogminclan     _ o _ _ _ _ i _ i _ _

11. umen     _ _ _ u

12. treien     e _ t _ _ _

13. teclayx     _ _ _ _ t _ y

14. tdapa     _ d _ _ _

15. stenba     _ _ _ e n _

16. grduinon     _ _ _ _ d _ n _

17. bismslpeeri     _ e _ _ i _ _ _ _ _ e

18. ucghat     _ _ u _ _ t

19. wearyl     _ _ w y _ _

20. tmaoinlpc     _ _ _ p _ _ a _ _

21. icmoc     _ _ m _ _

22. rstnecao     _ n _ _ _ t _ _

23. oteru     r _ _ _ _

24. alforv     _ _ a _ _ r

25. atcinap     c _ _ t _ _ _

26. oyuth     _ _ _ _ h

# 5th Grade Spelling Words

Score: _____

Date: _____

Write and circle the correct spelling for each word.

|    |                  | A | B | C | D |
|----|------------------|---|---|---|---|
| 1. | _____ | enttared | entered | enttered | entared |
| 2. | _____ | ignorant | ignurrant | ignurant | ignorrant |
| 3. | _____ | brilaint | brilliant | briliant | brillaint |
| 4. | _____ | wonder | wonderr | wunder | wunderr |
| 5. | _____ | horable | horible | horrable | horrible |
| 6. | _____ | horicane | huricane | horricane | hurricane |
| 7. | _____ | Aprryl | April | Apryl | Aprril |
| 8. | _____ | respirasion | respiration | resspiration | resspirasion |
| 9. | _____ | information | infformasion | infformation | informasion |
| 10. | _____ | crruel | croel | cruel | crroel |
| 11. | _____ | January | Janaurry | Janaury | Januarry |
| 12. | _____ | buttom | botom | bottom | butom |
| 13. | _____ | bicycle | bicicle | bicylle | bicicle |
| 14. | _____ | cumett | comett | comet | cumet |
| 15. | _____ | recieved | reseived | received | recyeved |
| 16. | _____ | students | sttudents | sttodents | stodents |
| 17. | _____ | movenment | movenmentt | movementt | movement |
| 18. | _____ | cumpay | cumpany | company | compay |
| 19. | _____ | disclike | disslike | dislicke | dislike |
| 20. | _____ | sheepish | shepysh | shepish | sheapish |
| 21. | _____ | surprise | surrprise | surprice | surrprice |
| 22. | _____ | politicain | polliticain | pollitician | politician |
| 23. | _____ | senator | senattur | senatur | senattor |
| 24. | _____ | endoy | enjoy | enjyy | enjuy |
| 25. | _____ | pattroit | pattriot | patriot | patroit |
| 26. | _____ | brruise | bruice | bruise | brruice |
| 27. | _____ | sleeve | sleve | seeave | tlave |

Score: _____

Date: _____

# 5th Grade Spelling Words

*Fill* in the blanks with the correct spelling word.

| reminded | yesterday | frozen | district | frilly |
| excellent | terrible | surface | scoop | Florida |
| present | extent | professors | numb | arrived |
| mistletoe | graduation | | | |

1. The ground is still _____.

2. We are planning a _____ party.

3. Your blue dress is so _____.

4. I will _____ out some beans into this bag.

5. The flower was near dead when it _____.

6. The ideas that Kevin had were _____.

7. This _____ will vote at the main office.

8. My hand was almost _____.

9. The picture _____ me of how much fun we had.

10. The _____ of the damage was unknown.

11. We will buy the teacher a _____.

12. The _____ was smooth and cold.

13. I told you about the test _____.

14. This program was created by _____.

15. My haircut looks _____.

16. My mom will hang _____ over the door.

17. _____ is a peninsula.

# 5th Grade Spelling Words

Score: _____

Date: _____

*Fill* in the blanks with the correct spelling word.

| | | | | |
|---|---|---|---|---|
| drank | personal | equipment | I've | heavy |
| Arkansas | spaghetti | direction | moral | twenty |
| exist | choose | Wednesday | growls | Japanese |
| junior | wouldn't | empty | | |

1. You will make _____ dollars per day.

2. My dog _____ at everyone.

3. We sat outside and _____ tea.

4. We have a _____ obligation to do the right thing.

5. There is an _____ lot for sale.

6. The painting is much too _____ to carry by myself.

7. She said we could have lunch on _____.

8. My favorite food is _____.

9. My uncle has a cabin in _____.

10. I didn't even know that they still _____.

11. There's no need to get _____.

12. My best friend is _____.

13. She is a _____ partner in the law firm.

14. Our _____ is old and broken.

15. A palindrome can be read in either _____ like the word mom.

16. I just can't _____ between these shoes.

17. He _____ tell the secret to anyone.

18. _____ always loved to walk on the beach.

# 5th Grade Health: The Food Groups

Score: _____

Date: _____

First, read the entire passage. After that, go back and fill in the blanks. You can skip the blanks you're unsure about and finish them later.

| produce | consume | yogurt | stored | bones |
| repair | water | portion | vitamins | fiber |

Eating healthy foods is especially important for children because they are still developing. Children's bodies require nutrition to develop strong, healthy _____ and muscles. You will not grow as tall or as strong as you could if you do not get all the _____ and minerals you require while growing.

Healthy food includes a wide variety of fresh foods from the five healthy food groups:

**Dairy:** Milk, cheese, and _____ are the most critical dairy foods, which are necessary for strong and healthy bones. There aren't many other foods in our diet that have as much calcium as these.

**Fruit:** Fruit contains vitamins, minerals, dietary fiber, and various phytonutrients (nutrients found naturally in plants) that help your body stay healthy. Fruits and vegetables provide you with energy, antioxidants, and _____. These nutrients help protect you against diseases later in life, such as heart disease, stroke, and some cancers.

**Vegetables and legumes/beans:** Vegetables should account for a large _____ of your daily food intake and should be encouraged at all meals (including snack times). To keep your body healthy, they supply vitamins, minerals, dietary fiber, and phytonutrients (nutrients found naturally in plants).

**Grain (cereal) foods:** choose wholegrain and/or high _____ bread, cereals, rice, pasta, noodles, and so on. These foods provide you with the energy you require to grow, develop, and learn. Refined grain products (such as cakes and biscuits) can contain added sugar, fat, and sodium.

**Protein** from lean meats and poultry, fish, eggs, tofu, nuts and seeds, and legumes/beans is used by our bodies to _____ specialized chemicals such as hemoglobin and adrenalin. Protein also helps to build, maintain, and _____ tissues in our bodies. Protein is the primary component of muscles and organs (such as your heart).

Calories are a unit of measurement for the amount of energy in food. We gain calories when we eat, which gives us the energy to run around and do things. If we _____ more calories than we expend while moving, our bodies will store the excess calories as fat. If we burn more calories than we consume, our bodies will begin to burn the previously _____ fat.

Consider the five food groups when making your grocery list: fruits, vegetables, grains, protein foods, and dairy or fortified soy alternatives. Examine the foods you already have in your refrigerator, freezer, and pantry, and then go shopping for any items you may be missing.

See if you can create a grocery list for each of the five food groups.

# Grocery List

### Fruits & Veggies
☐ potatoes
☐ tomatoes
☐ _____
☐ _____

### Refrigerated
☐ butter
☐ cheese
☐ eggs
☐ milk
☐ _____

### Frozen
☐ _____
☐ _____
☐ _____

### Packages
☐ cereal
☐ pasta
☐ rice
☐ soup
☐ _____
☐ _____

### Baking & Bread
☐ bread
☐ flour
☐ sugar
☐ _____
☐ _____

### Miscellaneous
☐ paper towels
☐ soap
☐ toothpaste
☐ _____
☐ _____

# Grocery List

### Fruits & Veggies
☐ potatoes
☐ tomatoes
☐ _____
☐ _____

### Refrigerated
☐ butter
☐ cheese
☐ eggs
☐ milk
☐ _____

### Frozen
☐ _____
☐ _____
☐ _____

### Packages
☐ cereal
☐ pasta
☐ rice
☐ soup
☐ _____
☐ _____

### Baking & Bread
☐ bread
☐ flour
☐ sugar
☐ _____
☐ _____

### Miscellaneous
☐ paper towels
☐ soap
☐ toothpaste
☐ _____
☐ _____

# Grocery List

### Fruits & Veggies
☐ potatoes
☐ tomatoes
☐ _____
☐ _____

### Refrigerated
☐ butter
☐ cheese
☐ eggs
☐ milk
☐ _____

### Frozen
☐ _____
☐ _____
☐ _____

### Packages
☐ cereal
☐ pasta
☐ rice
☐ soup
☐ _____
☐ _____

### Baking & Bread
☐ bread
☐ flour
☐ sugar
☐ _____
☐ _____

### Miscellaneous
☐ paper towels
☐ soap
☐ toothpaste
☐ _____
☐ _____

# 5th Grade Grammar: Sentence Building

Score: _____

Date: _____

Practice *sentence* building. *U*nscramble the words to form a complete sentence.

1. _____ ____ _____ you're _____ of.
   Show · us · capable · what

2. __ tried ____ _____ ____ _____ done ____ _____
   I · to · my · get · time. · homework · on

3. __ didn't know ____ _____ _____ to _____ _____ _____
   had · job. · I · decided · he · leave · his

4. _____ _____ _____ is _____
   Tom's · Mary. · closest · friend

5. __ _____ care ____ long ____ _____ _____ _____ it.
   comfortable · as · they're · I · don't · as · with

6. _____ bragged about _____ _____ _____
   Bob · big · his · boat.

7. _____ ____ _____ cloudy _____
   Does · look · it · today?

8. You _____ _____ you're ____ _____ _____
   know · my · friend. · already · best

9. _____ _____ each _____
   other. · Friends · help

10. Just _____ ____ _____ what's _____
    me · know · wrong. · let

11. _____ _____ took ____ _____ _____ things.
    off · Playing · my · mind · tennis

12. I _____ _____ ____ fun ____ _____ __ _____ songs _____
    thought · it'd · together. · a · sing · be · few · to

13. I'm _____ _____ ____ _____ candy.
    allowed · not · to · eat

14. _____ _____ it _____ _____ said?
    was · What · that · Tom

15. __ _____ _____ you _____ ____ _____ me.
    wanted · see · thought · that · I · to

16. _____ _____ _____ taste good ____ _____
    snack · all. · This · at · doesn't

17. I _____ _____ _____ _____ I _____ _____
    trombone · played · was · when · younger. · the

18. This _____ ____ _____ _____
    narrow. · road · is · very

19. _____ _____ _____ _____ tonight.
    later · see · I'll · you

20. _____ is _____ _____ where __ _____ _____
    I · the · born. · hospital · was · This

21. _____ _____ _____ _____ _____ in this _____
    there · many · library? · books · How · are

22. _____ _____ _____ blends _____ with _____ _____
    well · dress. · hat · red · your · The

23. _____ _____ _____ to your _____
    this · Attach · label · package.

24. __ owe _____ _____ _____
    time!  ·  I  ·  big  ·  you

25. ____ _____ _____ ____ _____ the _____ data?
    want  ·  overwrite  ·  you  ·  saved  ·  Do  ·  to

26. _____ loves ____ _____ ____ _____ shower.
    sing  ·  in  ·  to  ·  Tom  ·  the

27. The cement _____ _____ ____ __ _____ ____ _____
    a  ·  will  ·  couple  ·  of  ·  set  ·  hours.  ·  in

28. ____ my _____ home, __ _____ _____ ____ _____ friend.
    came  ·  across  ·  old  ·  I  ·  an  ·  On  ·  way

29. Teacher Zhang teaches _____ ____ _____ _____ ____ _____ _____ _____
    to  ·  at  ·  his  ·  day.  ·  every  ·  students  ·  Chinese  ·  school

30. _____ _____ this _____ ____ heart.
    learn  ·  sentence  ·  by  ·  Let's

31. _____ give _____ _____ and _____ _____
    directions.  ·  him  ·  detailed  ·  specific  ·  Please

32. _____ _____ them _____ _____ you?
    You  ·  well,  ·  pay  ·  don't

33. _____ _____ removed _____ _____ the _____ _____
    After  ·  the  ·  bandage,  ·  she  ·  subsided.  ·  irritation

34. __ can't believe _____ _____ _____
    already.  ·  it's  ·  Christmas  ·  I

35. I'm starting ____ understand _____ _____ _____ _____ ____ _____
    why  ·  want  ·  didn't  ·  to  ·  to  ·  you  ·  here.  ·  come

# Cursive Writing Practice

Score: _____  Date: _____

Why did the teacher wear sunglasses? (Because her students were bright!) Why was the teacher cross-eyed? (She couldn't control her pupils!) How do bees get to school? (By school buzz!) What did the paper say to the pencil? (Write on!) How do you get straight As? (Use

# Cursive Writing Practice

Score: _____  Date: _____

a ruler!) What building has the most stories? (The library!) What do you get when you throw a million books into the ocean? (A title wave!) What is snake's favorite subject? (Hiss-tory!) Why did the teacher write on the window? (To make the lesson very clear!)

# EASTER CROSSWORD

Easter, also known as Resurrection Day, is an annual spring holiday. It is a Christian celebration of Jesus Christ's resurrection from the dead. It is considered the most important day of the year by Christians. Non-Christians may observe Easter as the start of the spring season. Even if they do not regularly attend church, many people attend an Easter service.

Every year, Easter is not celebrated on the same day. This is known as a moveable feast. Currently, all Christian churches agree on how to calculate the date. Easter is observed on the first Sunday following the first full moon after March 21st. This means it takes place in March or April. It could happen as early as March 22 or as late as April 25.

# HEALTHY GREENS CROSSWORD

Humans have consumed leafy greens since prehistoric times. However, it wasn't until the first Africans arrived in North America in the early 1600s that the continent got its first real taste of dark green leafy vegetables, which they grew for themselves and their families. Cooked greens evolved into a traditional African American food over time. They eventually became essential in Southern regional diets and are now enjoyed across the country.

Dark green leafy vegetables are high in nutrients. Salad greens, kale, and spinach are high in vitamins A, C, E, and K, while broccoli, bok choy, and mustard are high in various B vitamins. These vegetables are also high in carotenoids, which are antioxidants that protect cells and help to prevent cancer in its early stages. They are also high in fiber, iron, magnesium, potassium, and calcium. Greens also have a low carbohydrate, sodium, and cholesterol content.

# Brain Teaser: Spot the Difference

1. You have to remember what you see in one picture and compare it to what you see in the other picture
2. You have to mark or circle the locations where you see a difference

Ready! Set! Go!

# Brain Teaser: Spot the Difference

1. You have to remember what you see in one picture and compare it to what you see in the other picture
2. You have to mark or circle the locations where you see a difference

Ready! Set! Go!

**FIND 6 DIFFERENCES**

# Brain Teaser: Spot the Difference

1. You have to remember what you see in one picture and compare it to what you see in the other picture
2. You have to mark or circle the locations where you see a difference

Ready! Set! Go!

# Brain Teaser: Spot the Difference

1. You have to remember what you see in one picture and compare it to what you see in the other picture
2. You have to mark or circle the locations where you see a difference

Ready! Set! Go!

ANSWER SHEET

# 5th Grade Science: Mallard Duck

First, read the entire passage. After that, go back and fill in the blanks. You can skip the blanks you're unsure about and finish them later.

| plants | habitats | female | bodies | quacking |
| North | hatch | foods | waddle | colors |

The Mallard Duck is what most people think of when they think of ducks. The Mallard is a common duck that can be found throughout __North__ America, Europe, and Asia. Central America, Australia, and New Zealand are also home to the Mallard Duck. Anas Platyrhynchos is the scientific name for the Mallard Duck. It belongs to the Dabbling Ducks family. Mallard Ducks enjoy the water and are commonly found near rivers, ponds, and other __bodies__ of water.

Mallard ducks can grow to be about two feet long and weigh about two and a half pounds. The __female__ Mallard Duck has tan feathers all over, whereas the male Mallard Duck has a green head, darker back and chest feathers, and a white body. Some people breed domestic Mallard Ducks in order to get different __colors__.

Mallards are omnivorous birds. This means that they consume both __plants__ and other animals. They primarily feed on the water's surface, consuming various seeds, small fish, insects, frogs, and fish eggs. They also enjoy some human __foods__, particularly grain from human crops.

Female Mallard ducks are well-known for their "quack." When you were a kid and learned that ducks make a __quacking__ sound, you were hearing the female Mallard. Females quack to attract other ducks, usually their ducklings. This call is also known as the "hail call" or "decrescendo call." This call can be heard for miles by the ducklings.

Like many other birds, Mallard ducks migrate in flocks from the north to the south for the winter and then back north for the summer. This way, they're always where it's warm, and there's food. These ducks are also adaptable in other ways. They thrive even when humans destroy their natural __habitats__. This is not to say that we should destroy their habitat, but they have not been endangered due to human interaction thus far.

Ducklings are young Mallards. A mother duck will typically lay 10 to 15 eggs. She cares for the eggs in a nest by herself. The mother duck will lead the ducklings to the water shortly after they __hatch__ from the eggs. They usually do not return to the nest after that. Baby ducklings are ready to go just a few hours after hatching. They can swim, __waddle__, feed themselves, and find food quickly. For the next few months, their mother will keep an eye on them and protect them. The ducklings will be able to fly and become self-sufficient after about two months.

# 5th Grade Grammar: Adjectives
## Matching

ANSWER SHEET

Adjectives are words that describe people, places, and things, or nouns. Adjectives are words that describe sounds, shapes, sizes, times, numbers/quantity, textures/touch, and weather. You can remember this by saying to yourself, "an adjective adds something."

If you need to describe a friend or an adult, you can use words that describe their appearance, size, or age. When possible, try to use positive words that describe a person.

| #  | Ans | Word | | Definition |
|----|-----|------|---|------------|
| 1  | O | disappointed | ⇢ | sad because something is worse than expected |
| 2  | K | anxious | ⇢ | worried |
| 3  | C | delighted | ⇢ | very pleased |
| 4  | G | terrified | ⇢ | very frightened |
| 5  | I | ashamed | ⇢ | feeling bad because you did sg wrong |
| 6  | H | envious | ⇢ | wanting something another person has |
| 7  | N | proud | ⇢ | feeling pleased and satisfied |
| 8  | F | shocked | ⇢ | very surprised and upset |
| 9  | A | brave | ⇢ | nothing frightens him/her |
| 10 | L | hard-working | ⇢ | has 2 or more jobs |
| 11 | B | organized | ⇢ | everything is in order around him |
| 12 | D | punctual | ⇢ | always arrives in time |
| 13 | J | honest | ⇢ | uprightness and fairness |
| 14 | E | outgoing | ⇢ | loves being with people |
| 15 | M | loyal | ⇢ | always supports his friends |
| 16 | P | reliable | ⇢ | one can always count on him |

ANSWER SHEET

# 5th Grade Grammar Review

1. His father is the coach of the team.
   a. his, father, team
   b. his, father, coach
   c. **father, coach, team**

2. David is driving to the beach.
   a. David, driving, beach
   b. David, driving
   c. **David, beach**

3. What are the PROPER nouns in the following sentence? My grandparents live in Florida.
   a. grandparents, Flordia
   b. **Flordia**
   c. My, grandparents

4. What are all the COMMON nouns in the following sentence? I have two dogs and one cat.
   a. cat, one
   b. **dogs, cat**
   c. I, dogs

5. Which sentence contains only one common noun and one proper noun?
   a. **These potatoes are from Idaho.**
   b. Casey is a talented singer and dancer.
   c. I live near the border of Nevada and Utah.

6. Which sentence contains the correct form of a plural noun?
   a. **The wolves chase a frightened rabbit.**
   b. The wolfes chase a frightened rabbit.
   c. The wolfs chase a frightened rabbit.

7. Which sentence contains one singular noun and one plural noun?
   a. The musician tunes her instrument.
   b. The conductor welcomes each musician.
   c. **The singers walk across the stage.**

8. Identify the collective noun in the following sentence.
   Derek is the lead singer in a band.
   a. singer
   b. **band**
   c. lead

9. Which sentence contains the correct form of a singular possessive noun?
   a. The boxs' lid is torn.
   b. **The box's lid is torn.**
   c. The boxes' lid is torn.

10. Which sentence contains one concrete noun and on abstract noun?
    a. **John feels anxiety about meeting new people.**
    b. The young boy plays with trains.
    c. The sand feels warm between my toes.

11. Identify the simple subject in the following sentence. The children are playing tag.
    a. tag
    b. **children**
    c. The children

12. Identify the simple subject in the following sentence.
    This computer belongs to my father.
    a. **computer**
    b. This computer
    c. father

13. Which sentence has an object of a preposition?
    a. Several passengers missed the flight.
    b. Seattle is a city in Washington.
    c. The boys are racing remote-controlled cars.

14. Identify the object of preposition in the following sentence.
    The are playing a game of cards.
    a. cards
    b. game
    c. of cards

15. Identify the subject complement in the following sentence.
    Mr. Smith is a talented poet.
    a. poet
    b. talented
    c. Mr. Smith

16. Identify the subject complement in the following sentence.
    Tulips and daisies are my favorite flowers.
    a. my
    b. flowers
    c. favorite

17. Identify the direct object in the following sentence. Tyler delivers newspapers each morning.
    a. newspapers
    b. morning
    c. each

18. Identify the direct object in the following sentence. We will paint the bathroom beige.
    a. bathroom
    b. paint
    c. beige

19. Identify the indirect object in the following sentence. Mr. Jackson gave the students their grades.
    a. grades
    b. students
    c. their

20. Identify the indirect object in the following sentence. Mrs. Parker bought her husband a new tie.
    a. new tie
    b. husband
    c. tie

21. In which sentence is paint used as a noun?
    a. These artists paint the most amazing murals.
    b. We need two cans of brown paint.
    c. Let's paint the bedroom light green.

22. In which sentence is sign used as a verb?
    a. I saw it as a sign of good luck.
    b. Joelle is learning sign language.
    c. Did you sign the letter at the bottom?

23. In which sentence is file used as an adjective?
    a. This file contains the detective's notes.
    b. Put these papers in a file folder.
    c. I use a file to smooth the edges of my nails.

24. Identify the direct address in the following sentence. This is your baseball bat, Kenny.
    a. Kenny
    b. baseball
    c. bat

25. Identify the direct address in the following sentence.
    Hector, did you buy more milk?
    a. Hector
    b. you
    c. milk

26. Objects of the preposition. Lee cried during the movie.
    a. Lee
    b. movie
    c. cried

27. **Objects of the preposition. The phone is on the table.**
    a. table
    b. phone
    c. none

28. **Direct Objects: Every actor played his part.**
    a. his part
    b. actor
    c. played

29. **Direct Objects: The crowd will cheer the President.**
    a. the President
    b. cheer
    c. crowd

30. **Examples of concrete nouns are:**
    a. flower, music, bear, pie,
    b. love, cars, them, went
    c. me, I, she, they

31. **Direct Address: Well certainly, Mother, I remember what you said.**
    a. you
    b. Mother
    c. certainly

32. **Direct Address: I heard exactly what you said, Pam.**
    a. Pam
    b. none
    c. you

33. **Collective Noun: A choir of singers**
    a. choir
    b. sing
    c. singers

34. **Collective Noun: A litter of puppies**
    a. litter
    b. puppies
    c. puppy

ANSWER SHEET

# 5th Grade Grammar: IRREGULAR VERBS

1. **Jen has (go) to the same school since first grade.**
   a. gone
   b. goned

2. **When she was 17, she (wrote) a book.**
   a. wrote
   b. written

3. **Rees' mother (drive) them to the cinema.**
   a. drove
   b. drived

4. **begin**
   a. began
   b. begins

5. **The pitcher (throw) a no-hitter yesterday.**
   a. thrown
   b. threw

6. **bear**
   a. bore
   b. beard

7. **After practice, they (take) us to dinner.**
   a. tooked
   b. took

8. **They (become) best friends in the fourth grade.**
   a. began
   b. became

9. **burnt**
   a. burn
   b. burns

10. **break**
    a. broke
    b. brokes

11. **caught**
    a. catches
    b. catch

12. **The boy (say) that his name was Jim.**
    a. says
    b. said

13. **The Titanic had (sink) by the time the rescue boats arrived.**
    a. sinked
    b. sunk

14. **The cartoon character had (shrink) to the size of a mouse.**
    a. shrinked
    b. shrunk

15. **creep**
    a. creeps
    b. crept

16. **Ree and Jim have (know) each other for two years.**
    a. known
    b. knewed

17. dream
    a. **dreamt**
    b. dreams

18. Have you ever (wear) a cowboy hat?
    a. **worn**
    b. worned

19. fall
    a. falled
    b. **fell**

20. After practice, they (take) us to dinner.
    a. taken
    b. **took**

21. Speak
    a. **irregular**
    b. regular

22. travel
    a. **regular**
    b. irregular

23. go
    a. regular
    b. **irregular**

24. Come
    a. **irregular**
    b. regular

25. Love
    a. **regular**
    b. irregular

26. Become
    a. regular
    b. **irregular**

27. work
    a. **regular**
    b. irregular

28. read
    a. **irregular**
    b. regular

29. Create
    a. irregular
    b. **regular**

30. We (bring) my dog to the park.
    a. **brought**
    b. brung

31. I (make) my mom a cake.
    a. makes
    b. **made**

32. We (drink) all the water.
    a. drinks
    b. **drunk**

33. One day, he (see) a new student on the bus.
    a. sees
    b. **saw**

34. The two boys have also (see) many movies together.
    a. looked
    b. **seen**

35. They (go) to six movies last summer.
    a. gone
    b. **went**

36. Have you ever (wear) a cowboy hat?
    a. weared
    b. **worn**

# 5th Grade Grammar: Singular and Plural

ANSWER SHEET

1. Which word is NOT a plural noun?
   a. books
   b. [hat]
   c. toys

2. Which word is a singular noun?
   a. bikes
   b. cars
   c. [pencil]

3. Which word can be both singular and plural?
   a. [deer]
   b. bears
   c. mice

4. Tommy _____ badminton at the court.
   a. [playing]
   b. plays
   c. play's

5. They _____ to eat at fast food restaurants once in a while.
   a. likes
   b. [like]
   c. likies

6. Everybody _____ Janet Jackson.
   a. know
   b. known
   c. [knows]

7. He ___ very fast. You have to listen carefully.
   a. spoken
   b. speak
   c. [speaks]

8. Which one is the singular form of women?
   a. womans
   b. [woman]
   c. women

9. The plural form of tooth is
   a. tooths
   b. toothes
   c. [teeth]

10. The singular form of mice is _____.
    a. [mouse]
    b. mices
    c. mouses

11. The plural form of glass is _____.
    a. glassies
    b. [glasses]
    c. glassy

12. The plural form of dress is _____.
    a. dressing
    b. [dresses]
    c. dressy

13. Plural means many.
    a. [True]
    b. False

14. Singular means 1.
    a. [True]
    b. False

15. Is this word singular or plural? monsters
    a. [plural]
    b. singular

16. Find the plural noun in the sentence. They gave her a nice vase full of flowers.
    a. they
    b. [flowers]
    c. vase

17. Find the plural noun in the sentence. Her baby brother grabbed the crayons out of the box and drew on the wall.
    a. [crayons]
    b. box
    c. brothers

18. Find the plural noun in the sentence. My friend, Lois, picked enough red strawberries for the whole class.
    a. [strawberries]
    b. friends
    c. classes

19. What is the correct plural form of the noun wish?
    a. [wishes]
    b. wishs
    c. wishy

20. What is the correct plural form of the noun flurry?
    a. flurrys
    b. flurryies
    c. [flurries]

21. What is the correct plural form of the noun box?
    a. boxs
    b. boxses
    c. [boxes]

22. What is the correct plural form of the noun bee?
    a. beess
    b. beeses
    c. [bees]

23. What is the correct plural form of the noun candy?
    a. candys
    b. candyies
    c. [candies]

24. Find the singular noun in the sentence. The boys and girls drew pictures on the sidewalk.
    a. boys
    b. drew
    c. [sidewalk]

# ANSWERS

Round each number to the nearest tens.

1) 712 → 710
   − 397 → − 400
   315      310

2) 428 → 430
   − 232 → − 230
   196      200

3) 716 → 720
   + 479 → + 480
   1195     1200

4) 514 → 510
   + 133 → + 130
   647      640

5) 935 → 940
   − 188 → − 190
   747      750

6) 481 → 480
   + 131 → + 130
   612      610

7) 798 → 800
   − 647 → − 650
   151      150

8) 484 → 480
   + 235 → + 240
   719      720

9) 939 → 940
   + 548 → + 550
   1487     1490

10) 692 → 690
    + 542 → + 540
    1234     1230

11) 414 → 410
    + 921 → + 920
    1335     1330

12) 224 → 220
    − 154 → − 150
    70       70

13) 321 → 320
    − 257 → − 260
    64       60

14) 295 → 300
    − 182 → − 180
    113      120

# ANSWERS

## Converting Feet and Inches

**Convert to Inches.**

1) 4 feet  11 inches  59 inches     5) 15 feet  9 inches  189 inches

2) 8 feet  4 inches  100 inches     6) 13 feet  7 inches  163 inches

3) 4 feet  6 inches  54 inches      7) 7 feet  6 inches  90 inches

4) 14 feet  5 inches  173 inches    8) 4 feet  3 inches  51 inches

**Convert to Feet and Inches.**

9) 5 feet  1 inch    61 inches      13) 4 feet  9 inches  57 inches

10) 9 feet  4 inches  112 inches    14) 1 foot  9 inches  21 inches

11) 11 feet  6 inches  138 inches   15) 13 feet  7 inches  163 inches

12) 10 feet  9 inches  129 inches   16) 15 feet 10 inches  190 inches

# Time Answer Sheet

What time is on the clock?  6:00

What time will it be in 4 hours and 20 minutes?  10:20

What time was it 1 hour and 40 minutes ago?  4:20

What time will it be in 3 hours ?  9:00

What time is on the clock?  12:40

What time will it be in 1 hour and 40 minutes?  2:20

What time was it 2 hours and 20 minutes ago?  10:20

What time will it be in 1 hour ?  1:40

What time is on the clock?  2:40

What time will it be in 3 hours and 40 minutes?  6:20

What time was it 1 hour and 20 minutes ago?  1:20

What time will it be in 4 hours ?  6:40

What time is on the clock?  6:20

What time will it be in 4 hours ?  10:20

What time was it 2 hours and 20 minutes ago?  3:60

What time will it be in 2 hours ?  8:20

ANSWER SHEET

# 5th Grade History: The Mayflower

First, read the entire passage. After that, go back and fill in the blanks. You can skip the blanks you're unsure about and finish them later.

| ship | sail | voyage | assist | settlers |
| passengers | illness | load | leaking | Cape |

In 1620, a __ship__ called the Mayflower transported a group of English colonists to North America. These people established New England's first permanent European colony in what is now Plymouth, Massachusetts. Later, they were named the Pilgrims.

The Mayflower was approximately 106 feet long, 25 feet wide, and had a tonnage of 180. The deck of the Mayflower was about 80 feet long, roughly the length of a basketball court. The ship had three masts for holding sails:

The fore-mast (in front)

The main-mast (in the middle)

The mizzen mast (in the back) (back)

On August 4, 1620, the Mayflower and the Speedwell set sail from Southampton, England. They had to come to a halt in Dartmouth, however, because the Speedwell was leaking. They left Dartmouth on August 21, but the Speedwell began __leaking__ again, and they came to a halt in Plymouth, England. They decided to abandon the Speedwell at Plymouth and __load__ as many passengers as possible onto the Mayflower. On September 6, 1620, they set sail from Plymouth.

The Mayflower set __sail__ from Plymouth, England, west across the Atlantic Ocean. The ship's original destination was Virginia, but storms forced it to change course. On November 9, 1620, more than two months after leaving Plymouth, the Mayflower sighted __Cape__ Cod. The Pilgrims decided to stay even though they were north of where they had planned to settle.

It is estimated that around 30 children were on board the Mayflower during the epic __voyage__ to America, but little is known about many of them.

They were children of passengers, some traveled with other adults, and some were servants - but having young people among the __settlers__ was critical to the Plymouth Colony's survival.

It is believed that when the colonists faced their first harsh winter of __illness__ and death in a new land, the children would __assist__ the adults by tending to the sick, assisting in the preparation of food, and fetching firewood and water.

While nearly half of the ship's __passengers__ died during the winter of 1620/1621, it is believed that there were fewer deaths among the children, implying that the struggling colony had a better chance of thriving.

ANSWER SHEET

# 5th Grade History: Native American Princess Pocahontas

First, read the entire passage. After that, go back and fill in the blanks. You can skip the blanks you're unsure about and finish them later.

| freedom | ransom | gravely | chief | princess |
| Jamestown | thatch | captured | spare | accident |

Pocahontas was the daughter of the Powhatan __chief__. Historians place her birth in the year 1595. Her father was not only the chief of a tiny tribe; he was also the chief of a big confederation of Native American tribes that occupied a considerable portion of eastern Virginia.

Despite her status as the chief's daughter, Pocahontas' childhood was likely similar to that of most Native American girls. She would have lived in a __thatch__ roof house, learned to build a fire and cook, foraged for food in the woods such as berries and nuts, and played games with other children.

When Pocahontas was about twelve years old, strange strangers from a distant land arrived. They were colonists of the English language. They founded __Jamestown__ on an island near the Powhatan lands. The Powhatan's interaction with the outsiders was uneasy. They traded with strangers at times and fought them at others.

Captain John Smith, the Jamestown settlement's captain, was __captured__ by some of her father's warriors one day. According to mythology, Chief Powhatan was about to assassinate John Smith when Pocahontas rescued him. She pleaded with her father to __spare__ the life of Smith. Her father consented, and Captain Smith was released.

After Pocahontas saved John Smith, the Powhatan's relationship with the settlers improved. They traded with one another, and Pocahontas frequently paid visits to the Jamestown fort to speak with John Smith. In 1609, after being injured in a gunpowder __accident__, John Smith was forced to return to England. The Powhatan's relationship with the settlers deteriorated once more.

English Captain Samuel Argall captured Pocahontas in 1613. He informed Pocahontas' father that he intended to exchange her for the __freedom__ of other English captives held by the Powhatan. The two parties engaged in lengthy negotiations. Pocahontas met and fell in love with tobacco farmer John Rolfe while imprisoned. Even though her father had paid the __ransom__, she chose to remain with the English. On April 5, 1614, at the chapel in Jamestown, she married John Rolfe. She gave birth to a son called Thomas around a year later.

Pocahontas and John Rolfe sailed to London a few years after their marriage. Pocahontas was treated like a __princess__ while in London. She wore ostentatious gowns, attended extravagant parties, and met King James I of England. She even met John Smith, whom she had assumed was dead.

Pocahontas and John Rolfe intended to return to Virginia through the sea. Regrettably, Pocahontas fell __gravely__ ill as they prepared to depart sail. She died in Gravesend, England, in March 1617.

ANSWER SHEET

# 5th Grade History: The Thirteen Colonies

1. The Dutch founded _____ in 1626.
   a. New Jersey
   b. **New York**

2. 13 British colonies merged to form the _____.
   a. United Kingdom
   b. **United States**

3. Roger Williams founded _____.
   a. Maryland
   b. **Rhode Island**

4. A colony is a region of _____ that is politically controlled by another country.
   a. **land**
   b. township

5. Middle Colonies:
   a. **Delaware, New Jersey, New York, Pennsylvania**
   b. Georgia, Maryland, North Carolina, South Carolina, Texas

6. Colonies are typically founded and settled by people from the ___ country.
   a. **home**
   b. outside

7. Southern Colonies:
   a. Maine, New Jersey, New York, Pennsylvania
   b. **Georgia, Maryland, North Carolina, South Carolina, Virginia**

8. Many of the colonies were established by _____ leaders or groups seeking religious liberty.
   a. political
   b. **religious**

9. New England Colonies:
   a. **Connecticut, Massachusetts Bay, New Hampshire, Rhode Island**
   b. Ohio, Tennessee, New York, Pennsylvania

10. George and Cecil Calvert established _____ as a safe haven for Catholics.
    a. Maine
    b. **Maryland**

11. The colonies are frequently divided into _____.
    a. **New England Colonies, Middle Colonies, and Southern Colonies**
    b. United England Colonies, Midland Colonies, and Southern Colonies.

ANSWER SHEET

# Understanding Questions- Answer Relationship

The question-answer relationship (QAR) strategy helps students understand the different types of questions. By learning that the answers to some questions are "Right There" in the text, that some answers require a reader to "Think and Search," and that some answers can only be answered "On My Own," students recognize that they must first consider the question before developing an answer.

Throughout your education, you may be asked four different types of questions on a quiz:

**Right There Questions:** Literal questions with answers in the text. The words used in the question are frequently the same as those found in the text.

**Think and Search Questions**: Answers are obtained from various parts of the text and combined to form meaning.

**The Author and You:** These questions are based on information from the text, but you must apply it to your own experience. Although the answer is not directly in the text, you must have read it in order to respond to the question.

**On My Own:** These questions may require you to do some research outside of reading the passage. You can use primary sources to help such as online research articles, books, historical documents, and autobiographies.

**Why is the question-answer relationship used?**

It has the potential to improve your reading comprehension.
It teaches you how to ask questions about what you're reading and where to look for answers.
It encourages you to think about the text you're reading as well as beyond it.
It motivates you to think creatively and collaboratively, while also challenging you to use higher-level thinking skills.

1. Literal questions with answers in the text are ____.
   a. Right There Questions
   b. Right Here Questions

2. These questions are based on information from the text, but you must apply it to your own
   a. The Teacher and You
   b. The Author and You

3. Answers are obtained from various parts of the text.
   a. Think and Search Questions
   b. Check Your Knowledge Questions

4. These questions may require you to do some research outside of reading the passage.
   a. On My Own
   b. Find The Author

**Note:** Because of QAR type questions in this book - when grading your students' quizzes, please keep in mind that some of the questions were purposefully designed to be found outside of the text in this book, requiring your student to conduct additional research outside of the text provided. Their answer may differ depending on the source they used to obtain it. If a student cannot match an answer based on their own independent research, have them write it out instead. Please take this into consideration when grading.

# Tyrannosaurus Rex

ANSWER SHEET

When grading your students' quizzes, please keep in mind that some of the questions here were purposefully designed to be found outside of the text in this book, requiring your student to conduct additional research outside of the text provided. Their answer may differ depending on the source they used to obtain it. If a student cannot match an answer based on their own independent research, have them write it out instead. Please take this into consideration when grading.

Tyrannosaurus Rex, one of the most famous and notable dinosaurs, is a theropod dinosaur. Many Tyrannosaurus fossils have been discovered, allowing scientists to learn more about how big it was, how it hunted, and how it lived.

Tyrannosaurus rex was a land predator dinosaur that was one of the largest. The T-rex could grow to be 43 feet long and weigh up to 7.5 tons. Because of its size and overall fearsome image, the dinosaur is frequently used in movies and films such as Jurassic Park.

Tyrannosaurus rex was a two-legged dinosaur. This means it could walk and run on two legs. These two legs were large and strong enough to support the dinosaur's massive weight. The T-arms, rex's, on the other hand, were relatively small. However, it is believed that the small arms were powerful to hold onto prey.

The Tyrannosaurus' massive skull and large teeth are among its most terrifying features. T-rex skulls as long as 5 feet have been discovered! Other evidence suggests that the Tyrannosaurus had a powerful bite that allowed it to crush other dinosaurs' bones easily when combined with sharp teeth.

The Tyrannosaurus Rex ate meat from other animals and dinosaurs. Still, it is unclear whether it was a predator (hunted and killed its food) or a scavenger (meaning it stole food from other predators). Many scientists believe the dinosaur did both. Much is dependent on how fast the dinosaur was. Some claim that the T-Rex was fast and capable of catching its prey. Others argue that the dinosaur was slow and used its fearsome jaws to frighten other predators and steal their prey.

There are numerous significant Tyrannosaurus specimens in museums around the world. "Sue" at the Field Museum of Natural History in Chicago is one of the largest and most comprehensive. "Stan," another significant T-Rex specimen, can be found at the Black Hills Museum of Natural History Exhibit in Hill City, South Dakota. Also on display at the American Museum of Natural History in New York, paleontologist Barnum Brown's largest Tyrannosaurus find (he discovered five in total). The only known Tyrannosaurus Rex track can be found at Philmont Scout Ranch in New Mexico.

---

Remember that there may be some **question-answer relationship (QAR)** questions, so please keep that in mind when answering the questions below.

1. The T-rex usually measures up to _____ and weighs as much as _____.
   a. 43 feet, 2 tons
   b. 43 feet, 7.5 tons

2. The Tyrannosaurus rex was a _____ dinosaur.
   a. quadrupedal
   b. bipedal

3. The T-rex is a member of the dinosaur subgroup _____, which includes all the flesh-eating dinosaurs.
   a. Thyreophora
   b. Theropoda

4. The Tyrannosaurus rex lived in North America between 65 and 98 million years ago, during the late _____ period.
   a. Cretaceous
   b. Triassic

5. Where could we find the only documented track of a Tyrannosaurus Rex?
   a. at Philmont Scout Ranch in New Mexico
   b. at the Field Museum of Natural History in Chicago

6. Which of the following is the largest and most complete T-rex specimen that can be found on display at the Field Museum of Natural History in Chicago?
   a. Stan
   b. Sue

7. The Tyrannosaurus had a life span of around _____.
   a. 30 years
   b. 50 years

8. It is one of the most ferocious predators to ever walk the Earth.
   a. Giganotosaurus
   b. Tyrannosaurus rex

9. Tyrannosaurus rex was also adept at finding its prey through its keen sense of _____.
   a. smell
   b. sight

10. Tyrannosaurus rex (rex meaning "_____" in Latin).
    a. king
    b. master

ANSWER SHEET

# Calvin Coolidge

When grading your students' quizzes, please keep in mind that some of the questions here were purposefully designed to be found outside of the text in this book, requiring your student to conduct additional research outside of the text provided. Their answer may differ depending on the source they used to obtain it. If a student cannot match an answer based on their own independent research, have them write it out instead. Please take this into consideration when grading.

1. **Calvin Coolidge was the _____ of the United States.**
    a. 30th President
    b. 31st President
    c. 29th President

2. **Calvin Coolidge served as President from _____ to _____.**
    a. 1923-1929
    b. 1929-1933
    c. 1913-1921

3. **He is also famous for ____ earning him the nickname ____.**
    a. breaking up large companies, The Trust Buster
    b. bing excellent in academic, schoolmaster
    c. being a man of few words, Silent Cal

4. **Calvin grew up in the small town of _____.**
    a. Plymouth, Vermont
    b. Staunton, Virginia
    c. New York, New York

5. **Calvin Coolidge signed the _____, which gave full U.S. citizen rights to all Native Americans.**
    a. The Dawes Act
    b. Indian Citizenship Act
    c. Indian Civil Rights Act

6. **Who was the Vice President under Calvin Coolidge's administration?**
    a. Charles Curtis
    b. Thomas Riley Sherman
    c. Charles Gates Dawes

7. **Coolidge gained national recognition during the 1919 _____ when he served as governor.**
    a. Boston Police Strike
    b. Baltimore Police Strike
    c. NYPD Police Strike

8. **Calvin died of a sudden heart attack _____ years after leaving the presidency.**
    a. five
    b. three
    c. four

9. **Calvin Coolidge became President of the United States after his predecessor, _____ died in office.**
    a. Warren Harding
    b. William Taft
    c. Herbert Hoover

10. **The _____ is a nickname for the 1920s in the United States as it was a time of hope, prosperity, and cultural change during President Calvin Coolidge's presidential term.**
    a. Roaring Twenties
    b. Gilded Age
    c. Reconstruction

11. **Which of the following words best describes President Calvin Coolidge's personality?**
    a. quiet
    b. adventurous
    c. talkative

12. **What was Calvin Coolidge's campaign slogan when he ran for President of the United States?**
    a. Keep Cool with Coolidge
    b. Coolidge, For the Future
    c. Peace, Prosperity, and Coolidge

# Charles Lindbergh

ANSWER SHEET

When grading your students' quizzes, please keep in mind that some of the questions here were purposefully designed to be found outside of the text in this book, requiring your student to conduct additional research outside of the text provided. Their answer may differ depending on the source they used to obtain it. If a student cannot match an answer based on their own independent research, have them write it out instead. Please take this into consideration when grading.

1. **Charles Lindbergh was born on _____ in _____.**
   a. February 4, 1902, Detroit, Michigan
   b. January 29, 1905, Minneapolis, Minnesota
   c. January 7, 1900, Lindberg, Germany

2. **Charles' mother was _____.**
   a. a doctor
   b. an aviator
   c. a schoolteacher

3. **On May 20, 1927, Charles took off from New York aboard his plane, the _____.**
   a. Spirit of St. Luke
   b. Spirit of St. Louis
   c. Spirit of St. Joseph

4. **_____ were pilots that traveled the country performing stunts and giving people rides at air shows.**
   a. Barnstormers
   b. Sports pilot
   c. Recreational pilot

5. **Charles died in _____ at _____.**
   a. August 24, 1976, Minneapolis, Minnesota
   b. August 26, 1974, Maui, Hawaii
   c. August 25 1975, Detroit Michigan

6. **In 1924, Charles joined the _____ where he received formal training as a pilot.**
   a. Army Signal Corps
   b. Army Air Service
   c. Army Aviation Branch

7. **Charles Lindbergh was named the first ever _____ by Time Magazine in 1927.**
   a. "Man of the Decade"
   b. "Man of the Year"
   c. "Man of the Half-Century"

8. **In _____, Charles became a Brigadier General in the U.S. Air Force.**
   a. 1954
   b. 1974
   c. 1929

9. **When World War II began, Lindbergh flew around _____ during the war and helped to test out new planes.**
   a. 50 combat missions
   b. 60 combat missions
   c. 40 combat missions

10. **Charles was awarded the _____ by President Calvin Coolidge and a huge parade was held for him in New York City.**
    a. Aerial Achievement Medal
    b. Air Force Achievement Medal
    c. Distinguished Flying Cross

11. **Charles contributed to the development of _____.**
    a. an air pump
    b. an artificial heart pump
    c. a water pump

12. **Charles was one of the best-known figures in aeronautical history, remembered for the first nonstop solo flight across the Atlantic Ocean, from New York City to _____, on May 20–21, 1927.**
    a. United Kingdom
    b. Italy
    c. Paris

ANSWER SHEET

# Fiji

1. Fiji, officially the Republic of Fiji, is an island country in the _____.
   a. Arctic Ocean
   b. North Pacific Ocean
   c. **South Pacific Ocean**

2. Bula, which means _____ in Fijian, is the first word you'll need to learn because you'll hear it everywhere.
   a. Welcome
   b. Good day
   c. **Hello**

3. What is the capital and largest city of Fiji?
   a. Lautoka
   b. Nadi
   c. **Suva**

4. What is the climate in Fiji?
   a. Dry
   b. **Tropical marine**
   c. Temperate continental

5. ____, ____, and _____ are the official languages of Fiji.
   a. English, Fijian, and Samoan
   b. Fijian, Māori, and Rotuman
   c. **English, Fijian, and Hindustan**

6. The native Fijians are mostly _____ and the Indo-Fijians are mostly Hindu.
   a. **Christians**
   b. Catholics
   c. Buddhist

7. The traditional cooking method in Fiji is called _____.
   a. ahima'a
   b. uma
   c. **lovo**

8. After 96 years of British rule, Fiji became independent in _____ but remained part of the British Commonwealth.
   a. May 10, 1977
   b. **October 10, 1970**
   c. June 11, 1970

9. The original settlers of Fiji were _____ and _____ peoples who have lived on the islands for thousands of years.
   a. Austronesian, Micronesian
   b. **Polynesian, Melanesian**
   c. Polynesian and Micronesian

10. _____ is a Fijian military leader who led a 2006 coup that resulted in his becoming acting president (2006–07) and later acting prime minister (2007–14) of Fiji.
    a. Ratu Epeli Nailatikau
    b. **Frank Bainimarama**
    c. Laisenia Qarase

11. Fiji was ruled by one military coup after another until a democratic election was held in _____.
    a. **September of 2014**
    b. October of 2014
    c. November of 2014

12. What are Fiji's two largest islands?
    a. Kadavu & Mamanuca
    b. **Viti Levu & Vanua Levu**
    c. Rotuma & Lomaiviti

13. What country owns Fiji?
    a. USA
    b. **British**
    c. Italy

14. What is one of the languages do people mostly speak in Fiji?
    a. **Fijian**
    b. Portuguese
    c. Chinese

15. Who came to Fiji first?
    a. Duchess explorer Eden Thomas
    b. **Dutch explorer Abel Janszoon Tasman**
    c. John J Walker of Fiji

16. Where did the the nickname "Fiji" come from?
    a. From the government
    b. From the people of Fiji
    c. **From the Phi Gams at New York University**

17. What is Fiji known for?

    tropical islands

18. What is the capital of Fiji?

    Suva

ANSWER SHEET

# 5th Grade Geography: Lebanon

When grading your students' quizzes, please keep in mind that some of the questions here were purposefully designed to be found outside of the text in this book, requiring your student to conduct additional research outside of the text provided. Their answer may differ depending on the source they used to obtain it. If a student cannot match an answer based on their own independent research, have them write it out instead. Please take this into consideration when grading.

1. Lebanon is a country in the _____, on the Mediterranean Sea.
   a. Middle East
   b. Western Europe
   c. Africa

2. Lebanon has _____ rivers all of which are non-navigable.
   a. 16
   b. 18
   c. 17

3. What is the capital city of Lebanon?
   a. Tyre
   b. Sidon
   c. Beirut

4. Lebanon has a moderate _____.
   a. Mediterranean climate
   b. Continental climate
   c. Temperate climate

5. When the Ottoman Empire collapsed after World War I, which country took control of Lebanon?
   a. France
   b. Britain
   c. Russia

6. When did Lebanon become a sovereign under the authority of the Free French government?
   a. November 26, 1943
   b. September 1, 1926
   c. May 25, 1926

7. What is the national symbol in Lebanon?
   a. Maple tree
   b. Pine tree
   c. Cedar tree

8. Lebanon is bordered by _____ to the north and east, _____ to the south, and the Mediterranean Sea to the west.
   a. Israel, France
   b. Japan, Korea
   c. Syria, Israel

9. Lebanon is divided into how many governorates?
   a. 7
   b. 8
   c. 6

10. The Cedar Revolution occurred in 2005, following the assassination of Lebanese Prime Minister _____ in a car bomb explosion.
    a. Fakhr-al-Din II
    b. Rafik Hariri
    c. Jabal Amel

11. The city of _____ is one of the oldest continuously inhabited cities in the world.
    a. Byblos
    b. Baalbek
    c. Beirut

12. Lebanon is divided into how many districts?
    a. 24
    b. 25
    c. 22

13. Lebanon's capital and largest city is ____.

Beirut

14. Lebanon was conquered by the ____ Empire in the 16th century

Ottoman

15. Lebanon is a ____ country.

developing

16. Lebanon gained a measure of independence while France was occupied by ____.

Germany

17. Lebanon supported neighboring Arab countries in a war against ____.

Israel

18. How old is Lebanon?

nearly 5,000 years of history

ANSWER SHEET

# 5th Grade Geography: Mountain Range

1. A _____ includes geological features that are in the same region as a mountain range.
    a. mountain passes
    b. mountain chain
    c. [mountain system]

2. _____ are smaller mountain ranges that can be found within larger mountain ranges.
    a. Hill ranges
    b. [Subranges]
    c. Micro ranges

3. The world's tallest mountain ranges form when pieces of the Earth's crust, known as _____, collide.
    a. core
    b. mantle
    c. [plates]

4. The tallest mountain range in the world is the _____ and the longest is the _____.
    a. [Himalayas, Andes]
    b. Andes, Mt. Vinson
    c. Mt. Everest, Manaslu

5. Mountain ranges usually include highlands or _____.
    a. [mountain passes and valleys]
    b. valleys and rifts
    c. mountain peaks and edges

6. The Andes Mountains are the world's longest mountain range, stretching approximately _____.
    a. [4,300 miles]
    b. 5,000 miles
    c. 2,000 miles

7. _____ is a scientific theory that explains how major landforms are created as a result of Earth's subterranean movements.
    a. Erosion
    b. [Plate tectonics]
    c. Sedimentation

8. The Himalayas run 1,491 miles across much of _____.
    a. Central Europe
    b. South America
    c. [Central Asia]

9. What is the highest peak in the Rocky Mountain Range that is 14,440 feet tall?
    a. Mt. Everest
    b. [Mt. Elbert]
    c. Mt. Mayon

10. The majority of geologically young mountain ranges on Earth's land surface are found in either the _____ or the _____.
    a. Alpide belt, Oceanic Ridge belt
    b. [Pacific Ring of Fire, Alpide Belt]
    c. Oceanic Ridge belt, Circum-Pacific Seismic Belt

11. The _____ runs somewhat parallel to the Rockies, but further west in the United States.
    a. [Sierra Nevada Mountain Range]
    b. Appalachian
    c. Himalayas

12. Mountains often serve as _____ that define the natural borders of countries.
    a. enclosure
    b. [geographic features]
    c. barriers

ANSWER SHEET

# 5th Grade Science: Endangered Animals

1. In 1973, an international treaty known as _____ was adopted as a far-reaching wildlife conservation measure.
   a. International Union for Conservation of Nature (IUCN)
   b. **Convention on International Trade in Endangered Species of Wild Fauna and Flora (CITES)**
   c. Wildlife (Protection) Act

2. _____ programs can help protect endangered species.
   a. Preservation
   b. **Conservation**
   c. Restoration

3. The Endangered Species Act was signed into law by _____ in 1973.
   a. John Dingell (D-Mich.)
   b. **Richard Nixon**
   c. Richard Pallardy

4. What percent of threatened species are at risk because of human activities alone?
   a. Below 50 %
   b. Almost 50 %
   c. **Roughly 99 %**

5. These animals are listed as critically endangered because they are primarily threatened by hunters who kill them for their horns.
   a. **Black rhinoceros**
   b. Oryx
   c. Antelope

6. Who wrote the Endangered Species Act and argued that "only natural extinction is part of natural order?"
   a. Julian Huxley
   b. Richard Nixon
   c. **John Dingell (D-Mich.)**

7. Species that only exist in captivity (for example in a zoo), are called _____.
   a. **extinct in the wild**
   b. extinct species
   c. critically endangered species

8. It is defined as any species that is at risk of extinction because of a sudden, rapid decrease in its population or a loss of its critical habitat.
   a. **Endangered Animals**
   b. Exotic Species
   c. Distinct Species

9. It is a law that protects endangered animals by taking into account any destruction to a species' habitat, whether it has been over-consumed, any disease or predation that threatens it, and whether any other man-made factors put it in danger.
   a. The Republic Act of 1947
   b. **The United States' Endangered Species Act of 1973**
   c. The Wildlife (Protection) Act of 1972

10. By the early 21st century, it could be said that _____ are the greatest threat to biodiversity.
    a. **human beings (Homo sapiens)**
    b. wild animals
    c. exotic plants

11. Choose the correct order of the level of risk, starting with the most threatened animal and working your way down to the least threatened.
    a. **Critically endangered, Endangered, Vulnerable**
    b. b.Endangered, Critically Endangered, Vulnerable
    c. a.Critically endangered, Vulnerable, Endangered

12. The most pervasive threat to species in the wild is:
    a. Unsustainable hunting
    b. **Habitat loss and habitat degradation**
    c. Disease

# FOOD CHAIN ANSWERS

1. In ecology, it is the sequence of transfers of matter and energy in the form of food from organism to organism.
   a. Food Sequencing
   b. Food Transport
   c. **Food Chain**

2. \_\_\_\_\_ can increase the total food supply by cutting out one step in the food chain.
   a. Birds
   b. Animals
   c. **People**

3. Plants, which convert solar energy to food by photosynthesis, are the \_\_\_\_\_.
   a. secondary food source
   b. tertiary food source
   c. **primary food source**

4. \_\_\_\_\_ help us understand how changes to ecosystems affect many different species, both directly and indirectly.
   a. Food Transport
   b. Food Chain
   c. **Food Web**

5. \_\_\_\_\_ eat decaying matter and are the ones who help put nutrients back into the soil for plants to eat.
   a. **Decomposers**
   b. Consumers
   c. Producers

6. \_\_\_\_\_ are producers because they produce energy for the ecosystem.
   a. Animals
   b. Decomposers
   c. **Plants**

7. Each organism in an ecosystem occupies a specific \_\_\_\_\_ in the food chain or web.
   a. **trophic level**
   b. space
   c. place

8. What do you call an organism that eats both plants and animals?
   a. **Omnivores**
   b. Herbivores
   c. Carnivores

9. Carnivore is from the Latin word that means \_\_\_\_\_.
   a. **"flesh devourers"**
   b. "eats both plants and animals"
   c. "plant eaters"

10. A food web is all of the interactions between the species within a community that involve the transfer of energy through \_\_\_\_\_.
    a. **consumption**
    b. reservation
    c. adaptation

11. Why are animals considered consumers?
    a. because they produce energy for the ecosystem
    b. **because they don't produce energy, they just use it up**
    c. because they only produce energy for themselves

12. How do plants turn sunlight energy into chemical energy?
    a. **through the process of photosynthesis**
    b. through the process of adaptation
    c. through the process of cancelation

13. Grass produces its own food from\_\_\_\_\_.
    a. animals
    b. **sunlight**
    c. soil

14. Each of these living things can be a part of \_\_\_\_\_ food chains.
    a. zero
    b. **multiple**
    c. only one

15. When an animal dies, \_\_\_\_\_ breaks down its body.
    a. **bacteria**
    b. grass
    c. sunlight

ANSWER SHEET

# 5th Grade Science: Temperate Forest Biome

1. _____ are found in Northern Hemisphere regions with moist, warm summers and cold winters, primarily in eastern North America, eastern Asia, and western Europe.
   a. Wild forests
   b. Rainforests
   c. [Deciduous forests]

2. How many types of forest biomes are there?
   a. 2
   b. [3]
   c. 4

3. Temperate forests emerged during the period of global cooling that began at the beginning of the _____.
   a. Medieval Era
   b. Paleozoic Era
   c. [Cenozoic Era]

4. Major temperate forests are located in the following areas, except for:
   a. Japan
   b. [Korea]
   c. Eastern China

5. What makes a forest a temperate forest?
   a. Temperature, Two seasons, Tropics, and Clay soil.
   b. Temperature, Climate, Wet season, and Loam soil.
   c. [Temperature, Four seasons, Lots of rain, and Fertile soil.]

6. The three main types of forest biomes are: the rainforest, the temperate forest, and the _____.
   a. [Taiga]
   b. Broad-leafed
   c. Coniferous

7. Many trees rely on _____ to get through the winter.
   a. temperature
   b. [sap]
   c. rain

8. Temperate forests are usually classified into two main groups, and these are: _____ and _____.
   a. Indigenous, Evergreen
   b. [Deciduous, Evergreen]
   c. Coniferous, Deciduous

9. Deciduous is a Latin word that means _____.
   a. "to subside"
   b. "to rise up"
   c. ["to fall off"]

10. Certain trees in a temperate forest can grow up to how many feet?
    a. 50 feet tall
    b. 90 feet tall
    c. [100 feet tall]

11. _____ forests are made up mostly of conifer trees such as cypress, cedar, redwood, fir, juniper, and pine trees.
    a. [Coniferous]
    b. Broad-leafed
    c. Mixed coniferous and broad-leafed

12. The animals that live in temperate forests have _____ that allow them to _____ in different kinds of weather.
    a. [adaptations, survive]
    b. conformity, thrive
    c. compatibility, survive

ANSWER SHEET

# 5th Grade Art: J. M. W. Turner

Joseph Mallord William Turner, also known as William Turner, was an English Romantic painter, printmaker, and watercolorist. He is well-known for his expressive colorizations, imaginative landscapes, and turbulent, often violent sea paintings.

On April 23, 1775, J. M. W. Turner was born above his father's barbershop in London, England. When Joseph was a child, he began to draw pictures. He enjoyed drawing outside scenes, particularly buildings. His father's shop sold some of his drawings.

He began attending the Royal Academy of Art in London when he was fourteen years old. He kept sketching and painting with watercolors. Many of his sketches were published in magazines. While he mostly drew buildings and architecture, he also began to draw some seascapes.

In 1796, Turner completed his first oil painting. Fishermen at Sea was the title. Turner gained a national reputation as a talented artist as a result of the painting's critical acclaim. Many people compared his work to that of other well-known painters.

Turner was captivated by the power of God in natural scenes, particularly the ocean and the sun. He would make numerous sketches in numbered notebooks, which he would then reference when painting in his studio. He frequently included people in his paintings, but they were small and insignificant compared to the power of nature around them.

Turner's work evolved, with less emphasis on detail and more emphasis on the energy of the natural phenomenon he was painting, such as the sea, a storm, a fire, or the sun. The paintings' objects became less recognizable.

The painting Rain, Steam, and Speed is an example of this. Light and mist are used to power the train engine as it moves down the track in this landscape of a locomotive crossing a bridge. The focus is on the color and changing light as the train passes through the landscape.

Many of Turner's later works are reminiscent of the Impressionist style of painting that would emerge in France in the coming years. Turner's work undoubtedly influenced artists like Monet, Degas, and Renoir.

Many art historians regard J. M. W. Turner as the most incredible landscape painter of all time. His artwork had a significant influence on many artists who came after him, including many impressionists.

1. Turner's later works are reminiscent of the ____ style of painting.
    a. Impressionist
    b. Watercolor

2. In 1796, Turner completed his first ____ painting.
    a. colored
    b. oil

3. Turner began attending the ____ of Art in London.
    a. Royal State University
    b. Royal Academy

4. Turner was born above his father's ____.
    a. mechanic shop
    b. barbershop

5. J. M. W. Turner was an English Romantic painter, ____, and watercolorist.
    a. teacher
    b. printmaker

6. Turner frequently included ____ in his painting.
    a. animals
    b. people

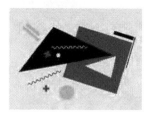

# 5th Grade Art: Abstract Art

ANSWER SHEET

1. Who splatters and dribbles paint directly from the can onto the canvas?
   a. Mark Rothko
   b. Jackson Pollock

2. Abstract Art consists solely of lines, ___, and colors.
   a. pictures
   b. shapes

3. Abstract Expressionism movement began in the 1940s in _____.
   a. Washington
   b. New York City

4. _____ created many large color blocks in his paintings.
   a. Mark Rothko
   b. John Mondrian

5. The main feature of abstract art is that it lacks a _____ subject.
   a. recognizable
   b. colorful

6. _____ paintings are filled with precision and geometric shapes.
   a. Mondrian's
   b. Rothko

7. The Abstract Expressionism movement began in the _____.
   a. The 1940s
   b. The 1840s

8. Based on what you read, what do you think is the main idea of abstract art?
   a. Not to tell a story, but to encourage involvement and imagination.
   b. Tell a true story and show emotions.

9. Who painted the first true Abstract Art in the early 1900s?
   a. Walter Kondiskny
   b. Wassily Kandinsky

10. Some abstract artists painted with emotion and _____.
    a. randomness
    b. black lines and dots

ANSWER SHEET

# 5th Grade Music: The Piano

Bartolomeo Cristofori was the first to successfully develop a hammer-action keyboard instrument and hence deserves to be regarded as the creator of the piano.

Cristofori was dissatisfied with musicians' lack of control over the harpsichord's loudness level. Around 1700, he is credited for replacing the plucking mechanism with a hammer and thus creating the modern piano. Initially, the instrument was dubbed "clavicembalo con piano e forte" (literally, a harpsichord that can play soft and loud noises). This was later abbreviated to the now-common term "piano."

The piano possesses the characteristics of both a string and percussion instrument. A hammer strikes a string inside the piano (much like a percussion instrument). The piano's sounds and notes are produced by the vibration of these strings (like a string instrument).

The piano is commonly referred to as a keyboard instrument. This is because it is performed similarly to several other keyboard instruments, including the organ, harpsichord, electronic keyboards, and synthesizers.

The organ was the first keyboard instrument, dating back to the third century. However, the organ did not begin to use keys until much later. The harpsichord was invented in the 14th century and quickly gained popularity throughout Europe. The harpsichord plucked a string and resembled modern pianos in appearance. However, plucking the string did not allow for the playing of various volumes and expressions.

The term piano is derived from the Italian phrase pianoforte, which translates as "loud and soft." This is because you may now adjust the volume of notes played on the keyboard.

The grand piano and the upright piano are the two primary types of pianos.

Grand piano - a grand piano's strings and primary frame are horizontal. This enables longer strings and also aids in the piano's mechanics. However, grand pianos can consume a significant amount of room.

Upright piano - This piano style is more compact, making it ideal for use in a home. The strings and mainframe are arranged vertically.

Additionally, there are electronic pianos. While the keyboard and playing technique is typically identical to a standard piano, the sound is frequently quite different.

1. This piano style is more compact, making it ideal for use in a home.
   a. Upright piano
   b. Downright piano

2. A ____ strings and primary frame are horizontal.
   a. organ piano's
   b. grand piano's

3. The term piano is derived from the ____ phrase pianoforte.
   a. English
   b. Italian

4. The ____ was invented in the 14th century.
   a. pianiochord
   b. harpsichord

5. The piano is commonly referred to as a ____ instrument.
   a. singer
   b. keyboard

6. The organ and harpsichord are keyboard instruments.
   a. organ
   b. guitar

ANSWER SHEET

# 5th Grade Music: Jimi Hendrix

First, read the entire passage. After that, go back and fill in the blanks. You can skip the blanks you're unsure about and finish them later.

| guitar | odd | acoustic | mother | Animals |
| guitarist | stage | Seattle | rock | childhood |

Jimi Hendrix, a __guitarist__, singer, and songwriter, wowed audiences in the 1960s with his outrageous electric guitar skills and experimental sound.

Jimi Hendrix began playing guitar as a teenager and grew up to become a __rock__ legend known for his innovative electric guitar playing in the 1960s. His performance of "The Star-Spangled Banner" at Woodstock in 1969 was one of his most memorable. Hendrix died of drug-related complications in 1970, leaving his imprint on the world of rock music and remaining popular to this day.

On November 27, 1942, in __Seattle__, Washington, Hendrix was born Johnny Allen Hendrix (later changed by his father to James Marshall). He had a difficult __childhood__, living in the care of relatives or acquaintances at times.

When Hendrix was born, his __mother__, Lucille, was only 17 years old. She had a rocky relationship with his father, Al, and eventually left the family after the couple had two more sons, Leon and Joseph. Hendrix only saw his mother on rare occasions before her death in 1958.

Music became a haven for Hendrix in many ways. He was a fan of blues and rock and roll and taught himself to play the __guitar__ with the help of his father.

When Hendrix was 16, his father bought him his first __acoustic__ guitar, and the following year, his first electric guitar - a right-handed Supro Ozark that he had to play upside down because he was naturally left-handed. Soon after, he started performing with his band, the Rocking Kings. In 1959, he dropped out of high school and worked __odd__ jobs while pursuing his musical dreams.

In mid-1966, Hendrix met Chas Chandler, bassist for the British rock band the __Animals__, who agreed to become Hendrix's manager. Chandler persuaded Hendrix to travel to London, where he formed the Jimi Hendrix Experience with bassist Noel Redding and drummer Mitch Mitchell.

While performing in England, Hendrix amassed a cult following among the country's rock royalty, with the Beatles, Rolling Stones, Who, and Eric Clapton all praising his work. According to one critic for the British music magazine Melody Maker, he "had great __stage__ presence" and appeared to be playing "with no hands at all" at times.

According to one journalist in the Berkeley Tribe, "Nobody could get more out of an electric guitar than Jimi Hendrix. He was the ultimate guitarist."

ANSWER SHEET

# A Community Garden Letter
# Questions

1. Who sent this letter?
   a. Andrew Fitzgerald
   b. [Jill Kindle]
   c. Dawn Clover

2. Who is the letter for?
   a. Jill Kindle
   b. Dawn Clover
   c. [Andrew Fitzgerald]

3. How much is the 10 x 12 plot per year?
   a. $90.00
   b. $45.00
   c. [$55.00]

4. What is Dawn Clover's phone number?
   a. 693-555-9006
   b. 963-555-9669
   c. [693-555-9009]

5. What job does Jill Kindle have?
   a. Community Garden Person
   b. [Director of Community Gardens]
   c. Garden Coordinator

6. What town or city is this community garden in?
   a. Gibbons
   b. Billings
   c. [Riverstide]

7. Where is the Greendale Community Garden?
   a. [678 Warren Drive]
   b. 780 Billings St.
   c. 789 Gibbons St.

8. How many plots are available?
   a. [2]
   b. 10
   c. 12

9. The water costs extra.
   a. True
   b. [False]

10. When was this letter written?
    a. [June 5, 2018]
    b. June 5, 2019
    c. June 9, 2015

ANSWER SHEET

# 5th Grade Reading Storytime: The Frog

When wishing was a thing, there was a King whose daughters were all __beautiful__, but the youngest was so stunning that even the sun, which has seen so much, was taken aback whenever it shone in her face.

A large dark forest lay close to the King's __castle__, and a fountain was hidden beneath an old lime tree in the woods.

Now, one day, the King's Daughter's golden __ball__ fell onto the ground and rolled straight into the water rather than into the little hand she was holding up for it.

When she turned around to the side from which the voice had come, she saw a __Frog__ sticking its thick, ugly head out of the water. "Ah! "Is it you, old water-splasher?" she asked, "I am weeping for my golden ball, which has fallen into the fountain."

"I don't care for your clothes, pearls, and jewels, or your golden crown," the Frog replied, "but if you will love me and let me be your __companion__ and playfellow, and sit by you at your little table, and eat off your little golden plate, and drink out of your little cup, and sleep in your little bed-if you promise me this, I will go down below and bring your golden ball up again."

He quickly came __swimming__ up with the ball in his mouth, and threw it on the grass. The King's Daughter was thrilled to see her pretty plaything again, and she quickly picked it up and ran away with it.

"Wait, wait," the Frog said. "Bring me along. I can't run as fast as you." But what good did it do him to scream his croak, croak, croak, croak, croak, croak! She ignored it and ran home, quickly forgetting the poor Frog, who was forced to return to his __fountain__.

The next day, as she sat at the table with the King and all the courtiers, eating from her little golden plate, something crept up the marble staircase, splish splash, splish splash. When it reached the top, it knocked on the __door__ and cried out:

She dashed outside to see who was there, but when she opened the door, the Frog was standing in front of it. Then she hurriedly slammed the door, sat down to __dinner__ again, and was terrified.

"Ah, dear Father, my golden ball fell into the water yesterday while I was sitting by the fountain in the forest, playing." Because I __cried__ so much, the Frog brought it out for me again.

ANSWER SHEET

# 5th Grade Spelling Words

Write and circle the correct spelling for each word.

| | A | B | C | D |
|---|---|---|---|---|
| 1. | grravity | grraviti | graviti | **gravity** |
| 2. | jewelri | jewellri | jewellry | **jewelry** |
| 3. | obstroct | **obstruct** | obsctruct | obsstruct |
| 4. | trompet | trrumpet | **trumpet** | trrompet |
| 5. | imigrant | imygrant | immygrant | **immigrant** |
| 6. | **oxygen** | oxygfn | oxyjen | oxyjtn |
| 7. | sensse | sence | **sense** | sensce |
| 8. | judje | juqje | **judge** | judne |
| 9. | altitode | alltitude | alltitode | **altitude** |
| 10. | **December** | Decemberr | Desember | Desemberr |
| 11. | **tolerable** | tolerible | tollerible | tollerable |
| 12. | acttive | actyve | acttyve | **active** |
| 13. | **aware** | awarre | awarra | awara |
| 14. | trryple | tryple | trriple | **triple** |
| 15. | exselent | excelent | exsellent | **excellent** |
| 16. | adaptible | adapttible | **adaptable** | adapttable |
| 17. | Ausstralia | Ausstralai | Australai | **Australia** |
| 18. | syngle | singlle | **single** | synglle |
| 19. | **launch** | luanch | laonch | loanch |
| 20. | smyled | smilled | **smiled** | smylled |
| 21. | finanse | **finance** | finense | finence |
| 22. | **climb** | cllymb | cllimb | clymb |
| 23. | introducsion | inttroduction | **introduction** | inttroducsion |
| 24. | Japanece | **Japanese** | Japanesse | Japanesce |
| 25. | speciallize | **specialize** | specailize | specaillize |
| 26. | gulible | **gullible** | gulable | gullably |

ANSWER SHEET

# 5th Grade Spelling Words

Unscramble the spelling words below.

Tip: Unscramble the words you are sure about first.

| afraid | entire | absent | caught | lawyer | ancestor |
|--------|--------|--------|--------|--------|----------|
| adapt | subordinate | permissible | freight | naughty | captain |
| flavor | complaining | feast | interact | compliant | rounding |
| comic | route | insects | youth | menu | exactly |
| Saturn | scissors | | | | |

1. osssicrs     s c i s s o r s
2. hgynatu     n a u g h t y
3. ifrgteh     f r e i g h t
4. aadrfi     a f r a i d
5. seaft     f e a s t
6. rtnsau     S a t u r n
7. itureabdnos     s u b o r d i n a t e
8. tetarnic     i n t e r a c t
9. scensit     i n s e c t s
10. ipogminclan     c o m p l a i n i n g
11. umen     m e n u
12. treien     e n t i r e
13. teclayx     e x a c t l y
14. tdapa     a d a p t
15. stenba     a b s e n t
16. grduinon     r o u n d i n g
17. bismslpeeri     p e r m i s s i b l e
18. ucghat     c a u g h t
19. wearyl     l a w y e r
20. tmaoinlpc     c o m p l i a n t
21. icmoc     c o m i c
22. rstnecao     a n c e s t o r
23. oteru     r o u t e
24. alforv     f l a v o r
25. atcinap     c a p t a i n
26. oyuth     y o u t h

ANSWER SHEET

# 5th Grade Spelling Words

Write and circle the correct spelling for each word.

| | A | B | C | D |
|---|---|---|---|---|
| 1. | enttared | **entered** | enttered | entared |
| 2. | **ignorant** | ignurrant | ignurant | ignorrant |
| 3. | brilaint | **brilliant** | briliant | brillaint |
| 4. | **wonder** | wonderr | wunder | wunderr |
| 5. | horable | horible | horrable | **horrible** |
| 6. | horicane | huricane | horricane | **hurricane** |
| 7. | Aprryl | **April** | Apryl | Aprril |
| 8. | respirasion | **respiration** | resspiration | resspirasion |
| 9. | **information** | infformasion | infformation | informasion |
| 10. | crruel | croel | **cruel** | crroel |
| 11. | **January** | Janaurry | Janaury | Januarry |
| 12. | buttom | botom | **bottom** | butom |
| 13. | **bicycle** | bicicle | bicyclle | biciclle |
| 14. | cumett | comett | **comet** | cumet |
| 15. | recieved | reseived | **received** | recyeved |
| 16. | **students** | sttudents | sttodents | stodents |
| 17. | movenment | movenmentt | movementt | **movement** |
| 18. | cumpay | cumpany | **company** | compay |
| 19. | disclike | disslike | dislicke | **dislike** |
| 20. | **sheepish** | shepysh | shepish | sheapish |
| 21. | **surprise** | surrprise | surprice | surrprice |
| 22. | politicain | polliticain | pollician | **politician** |
| 23. | **senator** | senattur | senatur | senattor |
| 24. | endoy | **enjoy** | enjyy | enjuy |
| 25. | pattroit | pattriot | **patriot** | patroit |
| 26. | brruise | bruice | **bruise** | brruice |
| 27. | **sleeve** | sleve | seeave | tlave |

ANSWER SHEET

# 5th Grade Spelling Words

*Fill* in the blanks with the correct spelling word.

| reminded | yesterday | frozen | district | frilly |
| excellent | terrible | surface | scoop | Florida |
| present | extent | professors | numb | arrived |
| mistletoe | graduation | | | |

1. The ground is still  **frozen** .

2. We are planning a  **graduation**  party.

3. Your blue dress is so  **frilly** .

4. I will  **scoop**  out some beans into this bag.

5. The flower was near dead when it  **arrived** .

6. The ideas that Kevin had were  **excellent** .

7. This  **district**  will vote at the main office.

8. My hand was almost  **numb** .

9. The picture  **reminded**  me of how much fun we had.

10. The  **extent**  of the damage was unknown.

11. We will buy the teacher a  **present** .

12. The  **surface**  was smooth and cold.

13. I told you about the test  **yesterday** .

14. This program was created by  **professors** .

15. My haircut looks  **terrible** .

16. My mom will hang  **mistletoe**  over the door.

17.  **Florida**  is a peninsula.

ANSWER SHEET

# 5th Grade Spelling Words

*Fill* in the blanks with the correct spelling word.

| | | | | |
|---|---|---|---|---|
| drank | personal | equipment | I've | heavy |
| Arkansas | spaghetti | direction | moral | twenty |
| exist | choose | Wednesday | growls | Japanese |
| junior | wouldn't | empty | | |

1. You will make __twenty__ dollars per day.

2. My dog __growls__ at everyone.

3. We sat outside and __drank__ tea.

4. We have a __moral__ obligation to do the right thing.

5. There is an __empty__ lot for sale.

6. The painting is much too __heavy__ to carry by myself.

7. She said we could have lunch on __Wednesday__.

8. My favorite food is __spaghetti__.

9. My uncle has a cabin in __Arkansas__.

10. I didn't even know that they still __exist__.

11. There's no need to get __personal__.

12. My best friend is __Japanese__.

13. She is a __junior__ partner in the law firm.

14. Our __equipment__ is old and broken.

15. A palindrome can be read in either __direction__ like the word mom.

16. I just can't __choose__ between these shoes.

17. He __wouldn't__ tell the secret to anyone.

18. __I've__ always loved to walk on the beach.

ANSWER SHEET

# 5th Grade Health: The Food Groups

Eating healthy foods is especially important for children because they are still developing. Children's bodies require nutrition to develop strong, healthy __bones__ and muscles. You will not grow as tall or as strong as you could if you do not get all the __vitamins__ and minerals you require while growing.

Healthy food includes a wide variety of fresh foods from the five healthy food groups:

Dairy: Milk, cheese, and __yogurt__ are the most critical dairy foods, which are necessary for strong and healthy bones. There aren't many other foods in our diet that have as much calcium as these.

Fruit: Fruit contains vitamins, minerals, dietary fiber, and various phytonutrients (nutrients found naturally in plants) that help your body stay healthy. Fruits and vegetables provide you with energy, vitamins, antioxidants, fiber, and __water__. These nutrients help protect you against diseases later in life, such as heart disease, stroke, and some cancers.

Vegetables and legumes/beans: Vegetables should account for a large __portion__ of your daily food intake and should be encouraged at all meals (including snack times). To keep your body healthy, they supply vitamins, minerals, dietary fiber, and phytonutrients (nutrients found naturally in plants).

Grain (cereal) foods: choose wholegrain and/or high __fiber__ bread, cereals, rice, pasta, noodles, and so on. These foods provide you with the energy you require to grow, develop, and learn. Refined grain products (such as cakes and biscuits) can contain added sugar, fat, and sodium.

Protein from lean meats and poultry, fish, eggs, tofu, nuts and seeds, and legumes/beans is used by our bodies to __produce__ specialized chemicals such as hemoglobin and adrenalin. Protein also helps to build, maintain, and __repair__ tissues in our bodies. Protein is the primary component of muscles and organs (such as your heart).

Calories are a unit of measurement for the amount of energy in food. We gain calories when we eat, which gives us the energy to run around and do things. If we __consume__ more calories than we expend while moving, our bodies will store the excess calories as fat. If we burn more calories than we consume, our bodies will begin to burn the previously __stored__ fat.

ANSWER SHEET

# 5th Grade Grammar: Sentence Building

Practice *sentence* building. *Unscramble* the words to form a complete sentence.

1. Show us what you're capable of.
   Show · us · capable · what

2. I tried to get my homework done on time.
   I · to · my · get · time. · homework · on

3. I didn't know he had decided to leave his job.
   had · job. · I · decided · he · leave · his

4. Tom's closest friend is Mary.
   Tom's · Mary. · closest · friend

5. I don't care as long as they're comfortable with it.
   comfortable · as · they're · I · don't · as · with

6. Bob bragged about his big boat.
   Bob · big · his · boat.

7. Does it look cloudy today?
   Does · look · it · today?

8. You already know you're my best friend.
   know · my · friend. · already · best

9. Friends help each other.
   other. · Friends · help

10. Just let me know what's wrong.
    me · know · wrong. · let

11. Playing tennis took my mind off things.
    off · Playing · my · mind · tennis

12. I thought it'd be fun to sing a few songs together.

    thought · it'd · together. · a · sing · be · few · to

13. I'm not allowed to eat candy.

    allowed · not · to · eat

14. What was it that Tom said?

    was · What · that · Tom

15. I thought that you wanted to see me.

    wanted · see · thought · that · I · to

16. This snack doesn't taste good at all.

    snack · all. · This · at · doesn't

17. I played the trombone when I was younger.

    trombone · played · was · when · younger. · the

18. This road is very narrow.

    narrow. · road · is · very

19. I'll see you later tonight.

    later · see · I'll · you

20. This is the hospital where I was born.

    I · the · born. · hospital · was · This

21. How many books are there in this library?

    there · many · library? · books · How · are

22. The red hat blends well with your dress.

    well · dress. · hat · red · your · The

23. Attach this label to your package.

    this · Attach · label · package.

24. I owe you big time!

    time! · I · big · you

25. Do you want to overwrite the saved data?

    want · overwrite · you · saved · Do · to

26. Tom loves to sing in the shower.

    sing · in · to · Tom · the

27. The cement will set in a couple of hours.

    a · will · couple · of · set · hours. · in

28. On my way home, I came across an old friend.

    came · across · old · I · an · On · way

29. Teacher Zhang teaches Chinese to his students at school every day.

    to · at · his · day. · every · students · Chinese · school

30. Let's learn this sentence by heart.

    learn · sentence · by · Let's

31. Please give him detailed and specific directions.

    directions. · him · detailed · specific · Please

32. You pay them well, don't you?

    You · well, · pay · don't

33. After she removed the bandage, the irritation subsided.

    After · the · bandage, · she · subsided. · irritation

34. I can't believe it's Christmas already.

    already. · it's · Christmas · I

35. I'm starting to understand why you didn't want to come here.

    why · want · didn't · to · to · you · here. · come

# ADDITIONAL ASSIGNMENTS PLANNER

○ MONDAY

○ TUESDAY

○ WEDNESDAY

○ THURSDAY

○ FRIDAY

EXTRA CREDIT WEEKEND WORK
○ SATURDAY / SUNDAY

GOALS THIS WEEK

WHAT TO STUDY

# ADDITIONAL ASSIGNMENTS PLANNER

○ MONDAY

○ TUESDAY

○ WEDNESDAY

○ THURSDAY

○ FRIDAY

EXTRA CREDIT WEEKEND WORK
○ SATURDAY / SUNDAY

GOALS THIS WEEK

WHAT TO STUDY

# ADDITIONAL ASSIGNMENTS PLANNER

○ MONDAY

○ TUESDAY

○ WEDNESDAY

○ THURSDAY

○ FRIDAY

EXTRA CREDIT WEEKEND WORK
○ SATURDAY / SUNDAY

GOALS THIS WEEK

WHAT TO STUDY

# ADDITIONAL ASSIGNMENTS PLANNER

○ MONDAY

○ TUESDAY

○ WEDNESDAY

○ THURSDAY

○ FRIDAY

EXTRA CREDIT WEEKEND WORK
○ SATURDAY / SUNDAY

GOALS THIS WEEK

WHAT TO STUDY

# GRADES TRACKER

| Week | Monday | Tuesday | Wednesday | Thursday | Friday |
|---|---|---|---|---|---|
| 1 | | | | | |
| 2 | | | | | |
| 3 | | | | | |
| 4 | | | | | |
| 5 | | | | | |
| 6 | | | | | |
| 7 | | | | | |
| 8 | | | | | |
| 9 | | | | | |
| 10 | | | | | |
| 11 | | | | | |
| 12 | | | | | |
| 13 | | | | | |
| 14 | | | | | |
| 15 | | | | | |
| 16 | | | | | |
| 17 | | | | | |
| 18 | | | | | |

**Notes**

# GRADES TRACKER

| Week | Monday | Tuesday | Wednesday | Thursday | Friday |
|------|--------|---------|-----------|----------|--------|
| 1    |        |         |           |          |        |
| 2    |        |         |           |          |        |
| 3    |        |         |           |          |        |
| 4    |        |         |           |          |        |
| 5    |        |         |           |          |        |
| 6    |        |         |           |          |        |
| 7    |        |         |           |          |        |
| 8    |        |         |           |          |        |
| 9    |        |         |           |          |        |
| 10   |        |         |           |          |        |
| 11   |        |         |           |          |        |
| 12   |        |         |           |          |        |
| 13   |        |         |           |          |        |
| 14   |        |         |           |          |        |
| 15   |        |         |           |          |        |
| 16   |        |         |           |          |        |
| 17   |        |         |           |          |        |
| 18   |        |         |           |          |        |

**Notes**

# End of the Year Evaluation

Name: _____

Grade/Level: _____ Date: _____

Subjects Studied: _____
_____
_____
_____

Cut out book

Goals Accomplished: _____
_____
_____
_____
_____

Most Improved Areas: _____
_____
_____
_____
_____

Areas of Improvement: _____
_____
_____

| Main Curriculum Evaluation | Satisfied | A= Above Standards<br>S= Meets Standards<br>N= Needs Improvement | Final Grades |
|---|---|---|---|
| _____ | Yes   No | 98-100 A+<br>93-97 A | _____ |
| _____ | Yes   No | 90-92 A<br>88-89 B+ | _____ |
| _____ | Yes   No | 83-87 B<br>80-82 B | _____ |
| _____ | Yes   No | 78-79 C+<br>73-77 C<br>70-72 C | _____ |
| _____ | Yes   No | 68-69 D+<br>62-67 D | _____ |
| _____ | Yes   No | 60-62 D<br>59 & Below F | _____ |

Most Enjoyed: _____
_____

Least Enjoyed: _____
_____

Made in the USA
Monee, IL
28 December 2022

23911643R00065